Healing Places

How people and institutions of faith can effectively address alcohol and other drug concerns

By Johnny Allem and Trish Merrill

ACKNOWLEDGEMENTS

The story of the Faith Partners Approach is a story of collaboration and grass roots innovation by dozens of congregations and hundreds of dedicated people. Their common bond is the hope and belief that brokenness is universal and recovery ever possible. The chronicle of this journey has likewise been nurtured and assisted by many. The authors are particularly beholden to our colleague Drew Brooks for his reporting on a case study, and Catherine Rush for her editing and advice. Our gratitude extends to JI staff who offered suggestions and encouragement, including George Bloom, Dona Dmitrovic, Ingrid Faust and Karen Jones.

ISBN 0-9759369-2-1

Table of Contents

Introduction

What most people perceive and understand as addiction is actually the final stages of addiction. It is true that our awareness of the disease usually begins in crisis. But the challenge facing society is to understand that illness commences early and raises recognizable symptoms—most of which are ignored. Most referrals to treatment come from judges, doctors, or employers, reacting to car wrecks, criminal actions, serious health failures, family breakups, or the job loss. The typical recovery story frequently starts with a crisis strong enough to jolt the alcoholic or addict into a "moment of clarity" and a willingness to seek help. Only then can the story continue with growth experiences restoring physical, mental and spiritual health.

Not all recovery stories need follow this common pattern. People with a propensity for addiction demonstrate symptoms long before the crisis stage. Their families may demonstrate difficulties and specific symptoms of family addiction even earlier, when everything else might seem "fine." These early warnings, unfortunately, are usually ignored, no matter how uncomfortable the individuals are with the problems and no matter how much damage is done—even when the damage is to children.

The work of Vernon Johnson and his colleagues who founded the Johnson Institute demonstrated that early intervention in the disease of addiction can be very successful. Dr. Johnson created and taught intervention technology to thousands of addiction counselors and related professionals throughout America and the world. This activity also demonstrated that early recognition and appropriate responses to these symptoms can be accomplished by a wide variety of professional and lay workers in education, primary health, public safety, and religious settings.

These ancillary professions must realize their stake in addiction illness and their opportunity to join in society's response if the path to addiction recovery is ever to begin before a crisis experience. Throughout America, professionals in schools, primary health care settings, welfare agencies, employer human resource departments, courts, public safety, and corrections have responded to this call.

In recent years, the Johnson Institute has fostered development of the team ministry model that engages lay congregational members in awareness, referral, and support for individuals and families afflicted and affected by alcohol and drug addiction. ("Afflicted" individuals directly experience addiction. "Affected" individuals are family members and close associates who are damaged in dealing with the person with addiction.) In pilot programs supported by the Johnson Institute and other organizations, the Faith Partners Team Ministry Approach was established in more than 150 congregations in several states. Research has demonstrated significant attitude changes, service outcomes, and specific instances of help for individuals and families in real need.

This book is the story of that work. The authors bring a passion drawn from the abundant restoration of human potential and a skill for contextual program design and teaching. Trish Merrill, a founder of Faith Partners, is a public health nurse with broad and varied experience in parish service and public policy. Johnny Allem, president of Johnson Institute, brings a career in journalism, business, government, and non-profit management, as well as his experience as a person with more than twenty years of recovery from alcoholism. Their connection to the subject includes familial ties, as well: Merrill is married to a minister, and Allem is a minister's son.

Together, we challenge America's institutions of faith to seize a unique opportunity to serve, nurture, and honor people troubled by the nation's number one treatable illness. This engagement requires much more than a simple acknowledgement of this significant population's existence. Healing places for individuals and families touched by addiction are successful when congregations learn facts, avoid judgement, practice love and provide supports.

Both the problem and the solution can occur in any faith institution of any faith tradition, no matter what the faith leader or the place of gathering is called. We use the word "ministry" for our Faith Partners Team Approach, though we know the word "service" would be more appropriate for some faith traditions. It is our hope and belief that the concepts explored here will begin new paths of understanding and service in thousands of congregations in the future. There is limitless potential in society today for Healing Places.

Trish Merrill

Johnny Allem

One

The Faith Team Idea

Why do we need ministries of recovery for people and families suffering from alcohol and other drug addiction?

One reason: they are here, in every congregation – lonely, frightened, uncertain, and ashamed. Some may know they need help and don't know where to turn. Others have yet to name their affliction but know something is wrong somewhere, perhaps in their own behavior or that of a parent, brother, or friend.

Unfortunately, most are not aware that addiction is a disease – a serious, progressive illness that requires intervention and treatment. Recovery requires abstinence, a surrender to a Higher Power, and working with others to overcome the obsession of dependency.

A key feature of the illness is that people who suffer are unable to diagnose themselves. After the first drink or drug, they lose all power to choose when and how to stop. Left alone, these individuals spiral into a private hell – usually ending in institutions or death, inflicting pain and suffering on all those close to them.

Public opinion surveys have demonstrated that pastors and places of worship are equal with doctors as the place people turn when faced with this devastating illness. Usually, it is family members who bring their questions and cry for help. Too often, their questions go unanswered. The pastor or church simply doesn't know what to do.

An understanding clergy supported by committed and trained members of the congregation have a tremendous opportunity to serve by addressing addiction problems in very early stages of pain. A ministry of recovery offers real hope: people with addictions get well, families heal, money is saved, life gets better, recovered people give back, congregations rejoice, and communities are safer. In short: everyone wins!

Many congregations are also home to individuals and family members already working toward addiction recovery – usually keeping their recovery secret. People often separate their recovery from their involvement in a congregation, keeping quiet out of a fear of being judged. A ministry of recovery offers them an opportunity to share their experience, strength, and hope without shame, to the benefit of those who still suffer and for the good of the larger congregation. It presents them with both a unique opportunity for service and the chance to pursue their own healing with the support of their congregational family. Through this work, congregations learn how science and faith live in harmony and how reaching out without judgment advances a healing climate for all.

Here are a few questions pastors and lay leaders can ask about their congregations when considering a team ministry devoted to addiction prevention and recovery in the congregation and in the community:

- What solace does our congregation offer those who suffer from alcohol and other drug addiction – their own or others?
- Do members of our faith community who have recovered from addiction disease feel safe talking openly about their experiences?
- How does our congregation prepare people young and old to make healthy decisions about alcohol and other drugs?

There's another reason that congregations find ministries of recovery both useful and uplifting: talking openly about alcohol and other drug addiction offers a context for talking about other addictions, for bringing all members of a congregation to a gradual awareness that it's not "us versus them." We are more alike than different – addicts all – looking for meaning, searching for God, and endowing false idols with power over our lives.

As the saying goes, "A church should be a hospital for sinners, not a museum for saints."

People go to their pastors for help when they hurt. They would go more often with alcohol- and drug-related problems if they knew their pastor and the congregation were sensitive to these problems and could respond to their needs.

Questions for the congregation:
- How often do weakness, failure, and fear come up in the dialogue of our congregation?
- What about the real problems of real people in coping with the tedium and unpredictability of daily living?

A ministry of recovery offers a congregation an opportunity to rejuvenate its spiritual life by talking openly about the hardship of daily living. In the context of practical healing, questions such as "Why I am here?" and "What is the meaning of my life?" get better scrutiny and more relevant attention. By struggling with such questions in community, a congregation offers its members support in their frailties, a place for their healing, and the tools for preventing new compulsions, addictions, or self-centered afflictions.

A team ministry defines recovery as:
- Recognizing addiction in us as well as others.
- Saying out loud, "Yes, this is something I need to deal with."
- Taking healing steps – sharing, finding information, seeking help, surrendering, and seeing God's work through others to provide a climate and means of healing.

Exactly what is a "ministry of recovery"?
Places of worship have always encountered the pain of those afflicted and affected by addiction. In recent years, as behavioral science has advanced and the healing role of faith been better identified, churches, synagogues, and mosques have begun crafting more specific outreach and services to those in pain.

The Faith Partners Team Ministry Approach examined in this book is a congregational team approach. Members with particular experience or interest in the healing process for people with addictions and the affected families join to advance healing opportunities within the congregation.

While one person can make a difference, involving a small group increases the impact enormously and makes the effort more sustainable. Supported by the clergy and endorsed by the full congregation, these teams conduct a sustaining service of healing. This service is three-fold:

- One, providing materials, events, and programs of education.
- Two, providing specific support, assistance, and referral to services for individuals and families in trouble.
- And three, recognizing, and honoring successful recovery.

Members of the team meet regularly, learn of community resources available to congregational members, consult regularly with the pastor, plan a calendar of appropriate educational opportunities, obtain and distribute helpful literature, meet with individuals referred by the pastor, and conduct events that celebrate recovery or enhance the congregation's climate of healing.

Most Faith Partners Teams undertake ministries of recovery and prevention. The usual strategy is to focus first on recovery because its principles of honesty, openness, and willingness are intrinsic to the spiritual growth and development of the ministry. That's also in keeping with where most teams start, with a core group of individuals in recovery who want to share their experiences with their faith communities.

Rev. Otto Schultz, a veteran Faith Partners organizer, describes the recovery work of ministry teams as "flashing their brights." When we see an oncoming car running without lights at night, all we can do is flash our brights to warn the driver, he says. We can't switch on the other's lights or take the wheel from the other driver.

The key contribution of a recovery ministry team is to flash a cautionary signal to the congregation. A team cannot and should not fix anyone. Its role as an agent of recovery is simply to offer members of a congregation an opportunity to look at their own lives and behaviors and, when they are ready, to help them seek out their own healing.

At the same time, by making the conversation an open one and allowing successful recovery to be seen and honored within the worship community, examples of healing are visible.

As agents of prevention, teams can make parents and concerned adults aware of their considerable sway over young people and provide them with tools and instruction to make the most of that influence. A significant body of research indicates that parents' communications of their values and expectations to their children reduces all kinds of risky behaviors, including drug and alcohol use.

Today's recovery ministry practice, as demonstrated in the Faith Partners Team Ministry Approach, has developed through years of experimentation, collaboration, and documentation. Congregational outreach was a feature of many addiction treatment centers when residential facilities became popular in the 1970s. The idea was developed by the Parkside Medical Services, a Chicago-based Lutheran network of 28-day treatment facilities.

At first, treatment centers approached churches simply as sources of referral. A philosophy of service and ministry to people troubled by addiction began to be identified and documented from this experience. John E. Keller, a pioneer in alcoholism treatment and one-time director of alcoholism services at Parkside, saw the opportunity for service to congregations in a wider context of prevention as well as recovery. His book *Alcoholics and Their Families: A Guide for Clergy and Congregations* demonstrates the possibility and power of healing that occurs in congregations when pastors and lay leaders work together to address addiction issues.

One of the Parkside-operated facilities during the 1980s was the Faulkner Center, in Austin, Texas. Trish Merrill began working at Faulkner in 1986 doing assessments with incoming clients. Her contact with Keller's philosophy provided a context for her own experience with the Twelve Step philosophy of recovery (many people, both affected and afflicted, work the Twelve Steps of Alcoholics Anonymous toward recovery as defined in the *Big Book of Alcoholics Anonymous* – see appendix for a copy) and her effort to integrate this healing process with congregational activities.

Merrill credited Keller's insights for "giving me the theology and language to make presentations to youth and adults about the healing power of addiction recovery."

Keller insisted that the church not take a moralistic or judgmental attitude toward addiction. He spoke of the universal tendency of human beings to get attached to something other than God when they experience the inevitable pain, brokenness, or sense of human limitation in their lives. He recommended that everyone understand that we are in the same boat – totally dependent upon the mercies of God.

People of all experiences can benefit from Keller's view. All lives face struggle. Struggles may differ, but there is no room for judgment. There is clear evidence that God sides with the outcast, the marginalized, the poor, and the sick. So it follows that those faithful to that vision would be led into a ministry with the poor, the sick, and the marginalized.

At the Faulkner Center, Keller and Therese Golden, a Dominican nun, introduced Merrill to the parish team model. They encouraged her to host an educational series for members of congregations so that clergy and church members would know about addiction disease and know about the services of the Faulkner Center. For three years, Merrill coordinated these classes. The Presbyterian Church made a video featuring two of the teams, which was entitled "An Elephant in the Sanctuary."

In 1990, with a grant from the Texas Commission on Alcohol and Drugs, Merrill began replicating the Austin model of congregational teams under the auspices of the Texas Conference of Churches. In the next five years, the project worked with more than 250 congregations in 19 communities, furnishing education through speakers, videos, and discussion. Topics included Alcoholism the Disease, the Family and Alcoholism, Other Addictions, Intervention, Prevention, and Recovery.

The strength in the project was the faith community's interest and eagerness to learn. Clergy and lay members soaked up the information. The weakness, however, was that few participants were very eager to take on the work of continuing the education and service.

Merrill and others in the project learned that the most passionate and predictable person to volunteer for this ministry was the person in recovery. His or her energy, interest, and sense of service were high. However, the experience of shame and stigma kept many from introducing or carrying through with this effort. They also struggled with how to share their recovery in a way that did not contradict the Twelve Traditions of Alcoholics Anonymous. (See appendix for the Twelve Traditions of Alcoholics Anonymous, or AA.)

A new idea emerged. Teams that were true cross-sections of the congregation, including both people in recovery and others interested in the issue, began to be successful. Working together, team members found ways to work out issues among themselves – including how to be effective in a particular congregation.

Another weakness that was evident was a lack of user-friendly tools and materials. Most of the education materials were borrowed from other programs. With the help of a retired newspaper editor, Merrill fashioned a 168-page manual. Providing teams with guidelines, sample materials, and ideas unique to the congregational ministry helped teams organize for service work as well as education.

Throughout the early experience of congregational faith teams in Texas, Merrill found that personal experiences of team members with recovery experience were essential to understanding and commitment. Her own early emersion in AA's Big Book and practice of the Twelve Steps became a pattern for others who had not personally experienced recovery. All team members seemed to benefit a great deal from attending open AA, Al-Anon, and other Twelve Step meetings.

It became clear that champions of this ministry, usually in recovery, see the work as a "calling." Most of them said that their church wasn't much help at the time of their need. They were determined that this ministry would make it easier for others to get help and reduce the shame.

Anita of Greater Mt. Zion Baptist Church in Austin was the first champion. Anita not only caught the vision, she began to develop the materials that every new team would want: a guide on what to say to the pastor; a brochure explaining this ministry; a description of necessary education; a handbook for team members, listing names and phone numbers; a protocal of what to say if someone calls; community resources; and announcements and prayers to be used in worship services.

Anita had been in the church for a long time and she saw the need to integrate this ministry fully into the life of the congregation. She was comfortable in asking for her pastor's blessing at critical points. Mostly she considered his early affirmation as permission to move on in creative ways.

Support outside of the individual congregation proved helpful to teams. One method of supporting teams was to host a statewide, three-day "Renewal of Teams" summer institute. The project conducted these institutes for two consecutive years, offering continuing education at a low cost to participants by using the facilities of a local university. People who had received team training came from all over Texas. Team facilitators led panel discussions and presented workshops on recovery and the Twelve Steps, prevention strategies, codependency, and intervention. Team members gained a renewed sense of purpose. They were inspired and motivated by one another and the presenters and left full of ideas for this relatively new ministry.

This project, known as Project ADEPT (Alcohol and Drug Education in the Parishes of Texas) laid much of the groundwork for what would become the Faith Partners Team Ministry Approach. The National Council of Churches recognized project ADEPT in 1994. Loss of state funding in 1995 ended the project – but not the work.

In Merrill's earliest efforts to learn and work with people facing alcohol and other drug issues, she served as a member of the San Antonio Council on Alcohol and Drugs. Two Minnesota professionals provided instruction that became her bedrock understanding of the disease. They were Dr. Vernon Johnson, who taught intervention skills, and Sharon Wegscheider, who presented an understanding of the effects of alcoholism on family members. Dr. Johnson, creator of the professional intervention strategy and founder of the Johnson Institute, was an Episcopal priest who devoted his life to the science and practice of addiction intervention and treatment following his own recovery from alcoholism.

It was the Johnson Institute that identified the work of Merrill and others in Texas in 1996 and provided the funding and support to continue crafting the Faith Partners Team Ministry Approach.

The Treatable Disease

The Alcoholics Anonymous (AA) response to alcohol addiction in the mid-Twentieth century offered a major milestone of hope for individuals and families afflicted and affected by this disease. For the first time in centuries, society held real hope that the tragic downward spiral of alcoholism could be reversed. From this experience, science and practice related to alcohol and other drug addiction advanced exponentially.

The AA response included three critical elements:

- First, alcoholism was described as an illness, affecting the body, mind, and spirit. It came to be defined as "a physical allergy and a mental obsession."
- Second, this information was transferred in person from one alcoholic to another which produced dramatic, positive results.
- Third, sustained recovery was best assured by actions that included spiritual, mental, and physical regimens.

The early discovery of the AA response centered on the experience of individuals who had suffered the extreme consequences of their addiction. There seemed a direct correlation between total exhaustion of self-will and the acceptance required to change physical, mental, and spiritual behaviors. A "bottom" was required for recovery to start.

The miracle of AA was not only that a "psychic change" could occur, allowing formerly hopeless individuals to recover, it was that this experience could be replicated over and over again when certain suggestions were followed.

Significant influence from medical, religious, and psychiatric authorities accompanied AA's birth and development. Dr. William Silkworth, Dr. Harry Tiebout, Father Dowling, Harry Emerson Fosdick, Emmit Fox, Carl Jung, and many others contributed to the AA suggestions and stories. Yale University established a fresh initiative of research into alcoholism which has steadily expanded over the years, yielding advances in knowledge as well as therapies and medicines.

The practical application of AA's discoveries, however, remained distant from the mainstream disciplines of medicine, religion, and psychiatry. The work of Bill Wilson, Dr. Bob Smith, and the "first hundred" people to achieve sustained recovery grew dramatically, but grew as a "stand alone" healing system – parallel to the health care system, parallel to churches, and parallel to psychotherapy. This disconnected aspect of society's response to addiction continued in the development of nearly all treatment options. The reluctance of churches to embrace and engage recovery is particularly interesting in that the great majority of Twelve Step meetings occur on church property, though with little linkage to church leadership or congregations.

As the years advanced, the major standing system of society to embrace and integrate recovery theories was the courts. Judges found AA's practical access and proven results useful to their immediate needs and consistently made referral to Twelve Step programs a standard feature of courtroom practice.

A system of recovery in America grew beyond the immediate practice of AA and other mutual support organizations. Formal treatment services were provided by government agencies and private sector organizations – profit and non-profit. Liberal insurance reimbursement for these services led to dramatic expansion from 1965 until 1995. Steep cost increases for primary health care and the resulting managed care practices sharply curtailed this reimbursement in the 1990s. At the same time, the public concurred with a punishing philosophy for behaviors associated with addiction, sending thousands of young people to jail and prompting the largest prison-building boom in the history of the developed world.

By 2002, public opinion in America reflected a new belief that alcohol and other drug addictions are primarily health problems, requiring health interventions more often than jail sentences. This belief that recovery happens broadly has allowed people to become contributing members of society. Americans are realizing that people with addictions and people in recovery are often their children, parents, co-workers, and neighbors.

The advancement in knowledge about addiction and its successful treatment, however, is out of step with society's current response to the problem. For more than 60 years, we have known that addressing the physical, mental, and spiritual needs of addicted people leads to recovery. We also know the rate of recovery increases dramatically when interventions occur earlier in a person's history of addiction and when treatments and recovery supports are extended in time.

In spite of this knowledge:

- Most people who have problems with alcohol and other drugs never confront the issue in their lifetime.
- Access to appropriate treatment is limited by commercial insurance practices, denying care to individuals despite contract provisions covering care.
- Appropriate responses to addiction normally occur around crisis – car wrecks, arrests for criminal behavior, accidents, health traumas, incidents of domestic violence. Early symptoms are ignored – even when they are abundant.
- Successful survivors are neither honored nor respected by society. Unlike survivors of other chronic illnesses, they are not considered resources. Rather, they face regular and systematized discrimination and are largely kept out of sight. Their usefulness to others is confined to practice within anonymous fellowships.
- Systems of treatment for alcohol and other drug addiction remain secluded and separated from traditional systems of care. Operating as a parallel system, addiction treatment facilities are not linked to primary health care facilities, schools, churches, or other standing institutions of the community.

One result of this mismatch between what we know and what we practice is that addiction remains an epidemic in America. We have the tools to transform this threat from a rolling epidemic to a manageable health risk. These tools have been effective with every other chronic illness facing our society.

First, recovery must be honored. Success in the management of chronic illness usually has two goals: help those who suffer from illness to recovery, and help reduce the frequency and severity of illness in the future. The function of people who succeed in recovery has traditionally been to participate and lead in efforts to conquer the disease. They demonstrate their success, their contributions to society are acknowledged, their joy is contagious, and they receive honor and respect from their community.

In the case of chronic alcohol and other drug addiction, society demeans the sick and ignores the recovered. Society's view of addiction is evidenced in discrimination throughout the experience. Victims are as likely to be jailed as treated. Most are ignored completely, spending their entire lives as family "secrets." The recovered are invisible as well. Though recovery is substantially a self-directed affair, the responsibility for public education, advocacy, and policy development rests largely with the treatment profession and community prevention activists motivated primarily by public safety.

Any successful strategy to make recovery a "probable" outcome of addiction illness, instead of a "possible" outcome, must begin by recognizing, honoring, and utilizing individuals with sustained wellness. Recovered people must move from being occasional witnesses to being leaders in a movement for widespread acceptance of proven recovery practices.

Congregations are uniquely qualified to advance this acceptance and utilization of people recovered from addiction – particularly those who rely on spiritual principles for their restored life.

Second, responses to the symptoms of addiction must be appropriate, timely, and accessible to all. The original AA experience found that an individual had to independently achieve a "bottom" of hopelessness before accepting new information. Vernon Johnson, an Episcopal priest who recovered from alcoholism, challenged this premise. With help from a congregational committee, he studied more than 200 cases of recovery to develop strategies of "early intervention." He created a technical process for helping someone troubled by symptoms of problem drinking to confront their issues and obtain professional help before losses of job, family, and home.

The Johnson Institute was founded to advance this "early intervention" technology, which consisted of enlisting family, business associations, pastor, and physician in the intervention process. Hundreds of thousands of people have experienced these "interventions," received professional treatment, and returned to their lives renewed, restored, and redeemed. A significant outcome of this technology has been the education of pastors, doctors, and employers.

Johnson Institute later developed job-site technologies for assisting troubled employees – resulting in the Employee Assistance Program movement. This work prepared the Institute for its support of faith-centered recovery assistance beginning in the mid 1990s.

The Johnson Institute model uncovered two important points: first, the efficacy of treating the illness at an earlier stage in the presentation of symptoms, and second, the existence of a family illness associated with the practicing alcoholic which makes it necessary to treat simultaneously the family and the alcoholic.

Today, even more advanced counseling and treatment technologies have proven effective for very early responses to problem drinking and drug use. Motivational Interviewing, described in the 1991 book by that name (Miller and Rollnick), expands on the ideas of early AA and Vernon Johnson, advocating a non-confrontational technology that is rich with counseling opportunities at every phase and stage of illness.

The experience of these new technologies has demonstrated that if responses to addiction were based on efficiency alone, society would demand that these responses occur in teen and early adult years and be addressed in a family context. Here again, an opportunity for congregational ministry is clear. A majority of Americans rely on church attendance at some point in their lives. Lives in trouble often display evidence of that trouble in church – though troubles related to alcohol and other drug use go undetected.

Third, all professions with a stake in addiction illness and recovery must participate in timely awareness of addiction and appropriate responses to it. Early response and intervention for people with problems related to alcohol and other drug use does not require new institutions, new professions, new buildings, or new administrations. Existing institutions of society that are in place and capable of responding to symptoms of addiction illness at early stages.

Places for more timely responses include schools, churches and other faith communities, work places, police departments, courts, welfare support systems, and correctional systems. Any and all of these professions can and must retool and retrain to participate in furnishing an appropriate response to alcohol and other drug consumption.

There is a direct relationship between volume and cost for each of these institutional opportunities. For instance, large numbers of people can experience intervention and early response at a low cost in elementary schools, high schools, colleges, and churches. At work places, interventions are often confined to people who perform poorly or cause problems on the job. If interventions happen when symptoms of trouble first occur, the initial costs for this intervention and treatment will rise. But capturing these problems early can reduce costs in the long run, not only saving the expense of more costly addiction treatment, but reducing the costs of general poor health and accidents.

Too often, sickness advances without intervention, and individuals eventually lose their jobs and enter public systems – either welfare-related or correctional. The interventions that occur when illness is most advanced result in responses that are very, very expensive. From society's point of view, successful models for handling chronic illness must focus on earlier response to wider numbers of people. That is the only way to reduce the costs of insurance, lost productivity, social services, and individual and family pain.

John E. Keller at Parkside Medical Services in Chicago developed a model for church initiative in providing responses to early symptoms of addiction illness in the early 1990s. As a Lutheran institution, Parkside sought ways to connect Lutheran congregations to the rehabilitative work of its addiction treatment center. Keller pioneered not only the concept of "faith team ministries," but a wider philosophy of lay service, pastoral counseling, and congregational support of healing for alcoholics and their families.

Fourth, public education must alert all citizens to their stake in both the tragic costs of addiction and the positive and frequent incidence of recovery. Stigma and discrimination hinder this strategy for overcoming addiction. Though most people recognize that addiction is a health condition, many deeply held beliefs indelibly stamp the alcoholic or addict as a social reject. Most discussions of addiction are negative, listing the dramatic costs to society of crime and other behaviors and the tragedy associated with individual and family deterioration.

Society needs new beliefs about addiction and recovery – ones based on truth and experience. Where better to establish new beliefs than places of worship?

Faith Partners Team Ministry address individual problems related to alcohol and other drugs, advancing churches as healing places.

Three
Removing Barriers to Healing

It is a few days before Christmas. Annette is looking forward to celebrating her third anniversary without drugs or alcohol. She is grateful, though lonely and a little conflicted.

Annette is 1,500 miles from home. She is 34 years old and a recent graduate from college, fulfilling one condition of her parole. With encouragement from her parole officer, she intends to enter law school and has learned how to deal with her conviction for selling drugs.

It is snowing outside and she is sharing her story at a Twelve Step meeting in the basement of a neighborhood church. It is not the church Annette regularly attends. She calls the group her "family," recognizing that her life has enjoyed three supporting families: her family of birth, her association with various churches, and her friends in Twelve Step programs. It is only with friends in recovery that all her secrets are shared.

She will not be going home for Christmas. Thanksgiving was a difficult time, with a brother drinking heavily and parents, though supportive, hoping she would soon be through with her "classes." She visited the church of her upbringing, the place she first mentioned her problem with drugs. The subject was just as "off limits" in her sobriety as it was when she was drinking and using.

The pastor who had prayed with her, but who did not know how to offer help, seemed to look past her, visibly uncomfortable and unable to say anything besides, "My, you're looking wonderful, Annette." She left the service feeling out of place.

Worship in church is important to Annette. This Christmas, she attended her new church in the city where she works, attends school, and found recovery from addiction. She found her new church home through a friend also in recovery, though neither of them has ever mentioned their addiction histories or their recovery in this congregation.

The relationships in this congregation are genuine and the pastor inspiring. This experience contrasts sharply with Annette's experience in early recovery. She had attended church in this new city for a number of years, though not regularly, and uncomfortably, given her growing use of alcohol and other drugs. After her arrest and experience in treatment, she found a path to recovery through attending NA (Narcotics Anonymous) and AA meetings.

She had no resistance to the need to pursue a spiritual path of recovery and was overjoyed to reconnect with a God she thought was beyond her. With great enthusiasm, she shared her experience with her pastor. Though kind and happy for her life without drugs or alcohol, he characterized her experience as sin and suggested she end her association with Twelve Step groups. She never went back to that church.

This all-too-common story illustrates barriers that diminish opportunities for healing in congregations. That these barriers exist in church, where troubled people most often turn for help, is a challenge for every person of faith. Challenging these barriers is the purpose of this book and the Faith Partners Team Ministries.

Whenever these barriers are broken down, opportunities increase for individuals and families to heal in a context of love and trust. Let's carefully review the barriers, then see how Faith Partners Team Ministries address them.

First, conversations about alcohol and other drug use, misuse, and addiction are rare and uncomfortable in most congregations. Though one in four families has direct experience with someone with an addiction experience, the subject is seldom raised. Though addiction disease strikes with equality individuals and families of every faith, every culture, every income level, and every community, a subtle taboo keeps the subject in the closet until a crisis occurs.

One result is that nearly all responses to addiction start at the point of crisis: a car accident, job loss, family breakup, violent act, criminal arrest. Our health care system is actually structured around meeting the illness at these crisis points. Even though addiction presents symptoms and causes problems in very early stages, our society ignores such warnings – at great cost and suffering to all.

Second, churches lack understanding of misuse or addiction to alcohol and other drugs. This shortcoming begins with pastors and extends throughout the congregational worship and service system. A recent study of faith institutions in the United States by Columbia University demonstrates that only 12 percent of America's pastors engaged in pastoral counseling have any training at all in addiction. The same study reports that ministers believe more than two-thirds of the issues they deal with in counseling have roots in addiction problems.

Clergy and congregational leaders, however, are not likely to admit their lack of knowledge and seldom make referrals to addiction treatment or traditional health systems in the community. Lacking understanding of addiction, pastors don't ask the questions or frame the conversation in a way that members would feel safe raising this issue. Others resort to their understanding of addiction as a sin. A context of judgment without appropriate medical assistance does little to assist healing or to encourage early discussion and intervention.

Third, individuals addressing their addiction issues fail to find a healing climate in most congregations. Though most successful pathways of recovery are spiritual in nature, traditional religious practice remains suspicious and circumspect with regard to Twelve Step and other spiritually centered programs. Many pastors view Alcoholics Anonymous and Narcotics Anonymous competitively and become jealous about participation in these programs. These views are nearly always associated with a lack of knowledge about the Twelve Steps.

Many congregations that do focus on addiction illness maintain a "separatist" attitude, continuing practices of isolation and discrimination.

Fourth, congregations are often unaware, and uninterested, in the tools of assistance available in the community. This is especially true of assistance related to addiction and mental health. This is a strange legacy for institutions with a long history of concern for physical health. Churches have historically founded hospitals, furnished volunteer health workers, and made bedside visitations a hallmark of pastoral service.

Few pastors or lay leaders have direct knowledge of where individuals can obtain medical treatment for addiction in their community, or where troubled families can get counseling, protection, or direct assistance.

Several national studies over many years have concluded that more than half of the hospital admissions for physical illness are related to misuse or addiction to chemicals. When "brief interventions" are engaged (short visits to make patients aware of the link between their illness or injury and intake of alcohol or drugs), readmissions to the hospital drop significantly.

These findings could significantly direct how pastoral counseling could be more beneficial in hospital settings.

Fifth, individuals who have succeeded in coping with their addiction experiences do not feel comfortable sharing their success within most congregations. This is in spite of the fact that most recovery stories are dramatic examples of spiritual healing, faith at work, and the special love of Providence in our lives.

People in recovery are not honored in traditional congregations, and they know it. Millions return to the faith of their childhood as a result of recovery yet hide the most significant fact of their healing and spiritual growth.

Sixth, the tremendous potential power of "congregating" is diminished when churches fail either to engage in a context of healing that assists people and families troubled by addiction or fail to honor successful recovery. Churches are one of the key venues where appropriate responses to addiction could change America's experience with addiction from an epidemic to a normal health threat. The other venues are work places, schools, primary health care facilities, and criminal justice agencies.

Let us now look at how a successful Faith Partners Team Ministries addresses these barriers:

Welcoming the conversation – Permission to openly discuss alcohol and other drugs, without automatic judgments, is the hallmark of a healthy and healing congregation. There is a saying in Twelve Step fellowships that "we are only as sick as our secrets." A climate of "permission" to share one's hurts, whether physical, emotional, or spiritual, is not an automatic endowment of religion. It must be cultivated and nurtured on a regular basis.

Understanding addiction illness – Congregations with an active Faith Partners Team Ministry have a broad awareness of the chronic, progressive nature of addiction illness. They believe recovery is a normal expectation when the disease is addressed. And they work to create a context of healing for everyone afflicted and affected by alcohol and other drug addiction.

This positive posture allows help to arrive for troubled families very early in the progression of either misuse or addiction to mood-altering chemicals. For instance, an educated and aware congregation often identifies troubled families through the behavior and concerns of children from that home.

Legitimizing a healing climate – Healing is neither an isolated task nor a spectator sport. Individuals are required to take personal responsibility for healing and wellness. Yet their progress is directly proportionate to the sharing they engage with those around them. In the most marvelous feature of spiritual healing, those in support of another enjoy healing as well. Everyone benefits from this climate and process. Everyone has the opportunity to be someone else's teacher or pupil on any given day.

The Faith Partners Team Ministry leads by example, coaching a response across the membership that serves all the membership.

Connecting with tools of help – Beyond nurturing an attitude of awareness, understanding, and healing, the Faith Partners Team Ministry conducts a community-resources survey. This survey identifies appropriate resources for a wide range of help and assistance that may be useful to congregational members. Linkages are established for direct medical care, counseling, housing, job training, and a host of other public and private resources.

Some of this research and outreach is conducted in concert with other Faith Partners Team Ministries in the community. This inter-faith networking adds another dimension of learning to the congregational service.

<u>Honoring recovery in individuals and families</u> – Recovery stories are powerful. Most congregational members with significant spiritual awareness recognize the power, the joy, and the beauty of these illustrations of grace. All people of faith can relate to human "brokenness" and the walk through pain toward wellness. Congregations with active Faith Partners Team Ministries identify and share the joy of recovery – not just of certain individuals and families, but of all God's children.

People in recovery, who have usually hidden their experience, are often the initial core of Faith Partners Team Ministries. One of the first benefits of opening the "conversation" about addiction within a congregation is the discovery of many people who already have positive experiences and joyful stories related to addiction recovery.

<u>Unlocking the power of congregating</u> – Great movements of civilization for justice, peace, and equality have been rooted in congregational celebrations of faith.

Throughout human history, people have recognized the power of community – achieving together what is impossible alone. We congregate around mutual beliefs as well as mutual need. And we nurture beliefs in stories, practices, and traditions that empower. Together, we find meaning in the transitions of life, value in our associations with each other, and treasure in seeing our daily lives in a spiritual perspective.

Healthy congregations demonstrate that life is spiritual with material aspects, rather than material with spiritual aspects. Wise pastoral leaders coach us to find moral strength within ourselves and validation in one another. More than any other institution of human endeavor, congregations are the channel through which we "change *the* world" by "changing *my* world."

Congregational action presents a vital opportunity for addressing America's number one preventable illness. It is here that the hurt, pain, and suffering of alcohol and other drug problems can best emerge as hope, faith, and love through successful recovery. Faith Partners Team

Ministries prepare a congregational context for healing, engage the hurting, point to direct help, nurture personal growth, and celebrate the victorious.

Four
Teams In A Healing Climate

It is God's intention for us to live in community. This broad belief is shared by all religions. It drives spiritual growth for individuals and congregations, directing us both inward and outward in our experience of healing and wholeness. In congregating, we learn of one another's healing gifts. In unity, we have the opportunity to engage a wounded world in need of healing. One minister has written:

"Health is not an individual achievement, but a community responsibility. Only those who share in the brokenness of others are whole."

A hallmark of congregations with successful Faith Partners Team Ministriess is a community that maintains a healing climate. The team is directed specifically to those afflicted and affected by alcohol and other drug problems – in every stage of illness and recovery. But the climate nurtures all manner of healing. Teams cannot work in isolation from the congregation. Healing cannot occur in a closet of the church. In some cases, a congregation with a healing climate encourages the development of a Faith Partners Team Ministry. In other cases, the actions and energy of a Faith Partners Team Ministry paves the way for a healing climate to grow throughout the congregation.

A congregational team ministry includes the team members, the team leadership, ministers within the congregation, the congregational membership, the larger community, and the network of other Faith Partners Team Ministries.

Team Members

Successful Faith Partners Team Ministries derive much of their strength from congregational members who enjoy recovery from addiction, even though they often keep this part of their lives secret from the congregation. Most are delighted to be able to speak openly of their experience and to find a place of service within the congregation. People who have benefited from a spiritual experience in their recovery find joy in being able to integrate the faith practices and experiences of their church and their recovery.

Other members bring their experience with loved ones, work associates, or close friends. They have found that the illness penetrates far beyond the person actually consuming addictive chemicals. People bend their behavior in response to alcohol and other drug addiction – often displaying symptoms of illness more rash or disturbing than those of the practicing drunk or addict. Many friends, associates, and family members survive and heal from their experience, even when the alcoholic or addict does not recover.

Professionals with experience in addiction illness are another source for team members. These may include counselors and therapists in the field, or health care practitioners with knowledge of the disease.

Many congregational members simply have a passion for helping people with chemical disorders and are drawn to this opportunity for service. Members who deal with children are often interested in becoming Faith Partners team members. They know that children often present the earliest symptoms of addiction in the family and present a unique opportunity for important service and healing.

Formation of a team ministry, then, usually begins with individuals finding a structure and method to serve others and celebrate healing. These beginning team members engage in two types of activity: first, they attend to their own healing; second, they assist others in the congregation.

Activities in the first category include fostering and experiencing the conversation about alcohol and other drug issues – both the problems and the recovery. Seeing this conversation emerge is often a moving and transforming experience – for people whose recovery stories are revealed and for members just learning about the prevalence of addiction issues as well as recovery in the congregation. Team members learn the science of addictive disorders as well as appropriate responses that include physical, emotional, and spiritual aspects.

In the second category of activities, the team members conduct congregational surveys, sponsor awareness and educational programs for all members, distribute appropriate literature, and make themselves available for individual assistance to families and church members in trouble. This category includes opportunities to learn new skills – both within the individual team and through inter-faith networking of Faith Partners Team Ministries in the area, region, or at the national level.

An important ingredient of both categories of work is the continued association with others and the healing that takes place through this interaction. "You can't give anything away that you don't have," is a spiritual concept that serves as a constant watchword in Faith Partners Team ministry.

Team Leadership

Faith Partners Team Ministries require minimal management and nurture relationships within and outside the congregation, helps the group set activity milestones, and leads the effort in a way that maximizes group and individual service. As in all new ministries and particularly in the launching of this unique team ministry, it is very helpful for the first leader to have several qualities or assets: a basic understanding of addiction, a positive relationship with the pastor, facilitation skills, a willingness to commit the time and energy and a comfort and maturity with their own life experience.

After the team ministry is established, leadership within the group can rotate, especially as the team recruits new members. This allows different experiences to be visible, better connection with the full group, and a sense of continuing renewal for the team at all levels. Leaders should consider themselves "coaches," not "bosses." The most important work of the team is the one-on-one association between team members and the full congregation. Leadership exists to support and enhance that activity.

Twelve Step fellowships consider their leaders as temporary and call them "trusted servants." This is a useful philosophy for Faith Partners Team Ministries.

Pastors

Faith Partners Team Ministries cannot be successful without the support and understanding of the church's ministers. In fact, pastors initiate many faith team ministries. Ministers regularly engaged in pastoral counseling are most likely to understand addiction and support the Faith Partners Team Ministry concept.

Many pastors in all religions, however, do not understand addiction. Nor are they aware of the extent of the problem, its impact on families and communities, or the number of people who have successfully recovered from addiction. Some may see it as a medical or societal problem to be dealt with outside the congregation. Others may respond in judgmental ways when problems with alcohol and other drugs emerge. Behavioral health issues are seldom addressed in seminaries or other forms of pastoral training. There may be resistance to accepting the science of addiction. National survey research (National Center for Addiction and Substance Abuse at Columbia University, NCASA, 2001) indicates that the majority of pastors do not consider that they are well prepared or sure of their role.

In addition, most pastors have heavy workloads and are not inclined to adopt new projects when they believe their workload will be increased or additional expenses to the church treasury are likely to result.

Pastors lend their support and help to these team ministries when (a) they understand that the teams will help reduce their work load, not increase it, and (b) they find the process of responding to symptoms of disease leads to healing for individuals and families. When congregational resources are available on one-on-one basis to support someone in trouble, provide personal stories of recovery, and make reliable referrals to appropriate community resources, pastors become enthusiastic supporters of the Faith Partners Team Ministry Approach.

Pastors participate in the work of Faith Partners by delivering a sermon focused on addiction recovery at least once a year and using the team resources in their daily pastoral counseling. They also participate regularly in awareness and educational activities of the team directed at the entire congregation, and they support use of a congregational survey.

The Congregation

Over time, a Faith Partners Team Ministry has an impact on every member of the congregation. It soon becomes known that it is safe to have an open conversation about chemical misuse or dependence in this particular church. As a result of a dedicated effort to make the congregation a "healing place," people with problems are served in a non-judgmental way. The congregation makes a habit of celebrating recovery and honoring those who have overcome their addiction experiences.

It is easy in the congregation to find the times and locations of the nearest meetings of Alcoholics Anonymous, Al-Anon, Narcotics Anonymous, and Nar-Anon. Specialized literature on questions faced by teenagers, young adults, and seniors are on display. Sunday School teachers who receive challenging questions know where to get answers.

Communities that allow healing from addiction to occur in their presence get the unique benefit of watching miracles happen before their eyes. The "faith that moves mountains" is no longer a rhetorical phrase, but a visible fact that reassures every worshiper.

The Neighborhood

The socially active church is linked to the larger community as a testimony to the practical aspects of spiritual living. Through a broad range of activities, from soup kitchens to housing for the homeless, America's religious institutions have traditionally demonstrated outreach to less fortunate citizens or those afflicted by disabilities.

The Faith Partners Team Ministry Approach extends this tradition in two specific ways.

First, its response to alcohol and other drug problems in the community is not condescending. By understanding the illness nature of addiction and the power and possibility of recovery, the congregation welcomes the broken as equals – understanding that at some level we are all broken. Sharing openly our brokenness is the first step of healing – for the troubled and for those who serve. The process of healing benefits all.

Second, many social problems and neighborhood pains are addressed when appropriate response to chemical misuse and dependence occurs. This appropriate response includes broad understanding, frank interventions early in the incidence of illness, and a family view of the disease that sees and acts on pain at its earliest point. Beyond providing alternatives and resources for those in crisis, the church becomes a beacon of information and awareness that exposes discrimination and reduces stigma.

The Faith Partners Team Ministry Network

Team members often report surprise and joy resulting from opportunities to meet and share experiences with Faith Partners teams from other neighborhoods, other faiths, and other cultures. These contacts usually occur at training sessions convened to share education and information across a region or state.

As mentioned earlier, continued growth and learning is essential to a healthy Faith Partners Team Ministries. In addition to stimulating creativity and service in leaders, continued education provides the opportunity to nurture developing leaders and assure constant renewal. Each session is designed to bring new tools, new understandings, and new skills to the team members.

The bonus benefit of these sessions, however, is what the team members share with each other. From shared experiences come binding relationships – often resulting in invitations for exchange visits between congregations.

The Minnesota Institute of Public Health conducted interviews with leaders from nineteen Faith Partners Teams in 2002. These congregations had participated in pilot versions of team development in Texas and Minnesota. The survey found that the average team consisted of seven members, with a consistent ratio of three males and four females. The ages of team members ranged from 16 to 86 years of age, with most being between 40 and 60.

Most teams meet on a monthly basis and include team members who are in recovery from alcohol and other drug addiction. The core teams are composed of diverse individuals, from business and legal people to high school and college students, from homemakers and retirees to healthcare and government workers. Besides the core team members, other members of the congregation help with special events.

The benefits of the team ministries cover a wide range of needs. According to the survey, team members reported these benefits:

- The team ministries have "opened up the conversations about alcohol and other drug problems" simply by being present in the congregation.
- Team members enjoy the opportunity to "give back" to the community.
- Working on the team promoted the member's personal recovery program.
- Important friendships were built as a result of team service.

Benefits to the congregation were reported as:
- The team is successful as a resource for people in need.
- The teams are a "symbol of hope" for the entire congregation.
- The service has helped attract new members to the congregation.
- The teams are a source of help and support for family members who may be suffering because of a loved one's addiction.
- The ministry offers a safe place to talk about the "feelings of shame that often accompany the disease and recovery process."
- As a result of the team activity, the whole congregation has "broken down barriers and diminished fears about addiction."

One team member told the survey, "The congregation can realize that no matter how perfect someone looks, they may be suffering and have pain." The team ministry helps everyone in the congregation see one another in a new way.

The leaders also reported "one size does not fit all." The Faith Partners Approach allows individual tailoring to each congregation. In the few cases where teams did not survive, members continued to express passion and willingness to pursue the team goals. Lack of clergy support or poor team leadership seemed to mark the efforts that were discontinued.

Five
Organizing A Team Ministry

Experience in developing the Faith Partners Team Ministry Approach demonstrated that teams with successful experiences year after year were always the ones with members representing a broad cross-section of their congregation. The survival and long service of a team depends on bringing together individuals of many different experiences, skills, and interests to provide a ministry that is appreciated and understood by the congregation. A healthy mix of talent helps establish a system of service that is larger and more sustainable than the popularity or tenacity of a single individual or group of individuals.

In Twelve Step language, this is called building with principles over personalities. There is a direct relationship between the time invested in organizing and building a team and the character and institutional nature of the emerging ministry. The more time and care invested in the foundation, the longer and stronger the team will be in years to come. There is no need to rush the steps required in organizing a team. Time is an important and essential ingredient for the task.

In this chapter, we will discuss:
• Finding willing partners.
• Learning about addiction.
• Identifying a facilitator.
• Talking with the pastor.
• Holding an exploratory meeting.

Finding Willing Partners

Addiction is a penetrating disease, leaving scars on one in four American families. It is very likely, then, that many people within any congregation are willing partners in an effort to engage healing and support healthy recovery. The job is to find them. They don't wear signs.

You may be thinking of this task yourself, reading this book in preparation for your own decision to serve. You may know of no one in your congregation who would share your interest. Not to worry. If you know the healing power of recovery and are reading this book, you have all the tools necessary to succeed. You need to carry out four steps to locate people who share your passion and can help construct a relevant mission for your team:

• Start conversations.
• Tell stories.
• Find common themes.
• Target mutual goals.

People have used this four-step organizing process to make friends, find food, sell cars, run for President, and all manner of social interchange since civilization began. It is useful to begin engaging people who are already in established congregational networks. For instance, having conversations with Sunday School teachers automatically broadens the scope of story telling and the opportunity to identify willing partners.

Converse with everyone you can. The quickest way to engage someone in conversation is to ask a question. Most people are willing to talk about themselves, their experiences, and their opinions. Here are some questions to ask:

• Do you know anyone who has recovered from addiction?
• If drinking in the family bothered a teenager, do you think he or she would share those feelings in church?
• Do you know where an AA meeting is? or another recovery support program?

Get the idea? Now be ready with your story. You must have a story, or you wouldn't be reading this book. A story does not have to be dramatic.

It just has to be real. "What comes from the heart, reaches the heart." Something a person says will enable you to share why you are interested in prevention or recovery aspects of chemical misuse and dependency. People find stories compelling and they match them with their own. That is what makes conversations work. In telling these stories, we tell a lot about ourselves.

When each of you have shared your stories, look for the interests you have in common, based on the story material. Asking about someone's feelings resulting from shared experience is often a good way to expand the sharing. For instance, you might say "You must be feeling sad (powerless, glad, grateful) as a result of …." It doesn't matter if you have guessed correctly or not.

Identify the common threads and apply them to current issues or actions. Put the issue into action language. "Our teens could learn better how to withstand peer pressure, don't you agree?"

From this stage in the conversation, you can ask for direct interest: "I have been studying a project that many churches have found useful in helping their children face difficult choices in life – particularly when it comes to drinking and smoking. How do you think a project like that would go over in our church?" Always ask the person's opinion on the idea first. Wait for their opinion before you ask them if they would personally like to be involved.

If the subject just doesn't connect with a person, let it drop. The goal is to find willing people, not to convert the unwilling. Using these steps, you should be able to find six or seven people from different perspectives and experiences in two or three weekends of conversation. Make notes about people who are willing. Note their personal experience, their views, and their skills. Don't forget the more mundane, such as the correct spelling of their name, their phone numbers and addresses.

Keeping in mind the importance of building a cross-section of interest and participation in the congregation, target conversations among these four categories within the membership of a faith community:

1. People in recovery – individuals who have healed and grown out of their experiences with their own or others' addiction.

2. Professionals in the field of chemical dependency or anyone who has received special training, including teachers, school counselors, and people working in employee assistance programs for major employers.
3. Parents and grandparents whose concern stems from love for the young people in their lives.
4. Clergy and church staff who have people asking them for help.

Learning About Addiction Recovery

There are ample means for learning about the various aspects of addiction: awareness, intervention, treatment, and recovery. A unique opportunity for team building exists, however, in learning together.

Attending open Twelve Step meetings together is both a learning experience and a sharing experience. Many teams ask new members to attend at least six support meetings. This can lead to internal discussions of the Twelve Steps, sharing recovery literature, and downloading information from a variety of prevention, treatment, and recovery websites. Individuals or groups can also attend formal and informal briefings, seminars, and training sessions that are often available in the community. Most are free of charge.

Establishing a relationship with community resources during the education phase of team building is very useful. Most communities have government and private agencies charged with responding to addiction issues. The government agencies will be listed under the phone book's government listings. Look for offices with "alcoholism" or "drug addiction" in the title, usually under health and welfare categories. Call the main number, and ask for the office of the director. Explain your interest and the interest in the congregation's potential Faith Partners Team Ministry. Ask for information about alcohol and other drug problems in your community and information on the services available.

Private agencies can be located in most yellow pages of your telephone directory. Look under the listings for alcoholism, drug addiction, behavioral health services, substance abuse, and youth services. Identify organizations that seem to have public information as well as public service missions. Call the director's office for education and information materials.

Visits to these agencies are useful. When two or three team members tour an agency together they usually get more out of the visit than one person would alone.

Here are three good books for getting both a general and a faith-based perspective on addiction, recovery/healing and prevention:

1. *Alcoholics and Their Families: A Guide for Clergy and Congregations* (John Keller).
2. *Parenting for Prevention* (David Wilmes)
3. *Thirst: God and the Alcoholic Experience* (James B. Nelson)

As you and your friends pursue the facts about the harm of misuse and addiction to drugs and alcohol, remember to find facts about the positive side of this disease. Some material is available on sites for national organizations supporting recovery. A good start is the site for the Faces and Voices of Recovery Campaign, www.facesandvoicesofrecovery.org, or the Johnson Institute, www.johnsoninstitute.org.

The best way to balance all the negative information about the sickness side of addiction is to get to know people who are experiencing recovery, including care providers and professionals who work in the prevention, treatment, and recovery field. You can meet these people in your visitation research as well as through contacts developed at meetings of Twelve Step and other recovery and support programs.

Identifying a Facilitator

The "lead person" in a Faith Partners Team Ministry is the facilitator, usually of the "lower case" variety. Since the key characteristic of a successful team is its ability to draw support and activism from all parts of the congregation, and people from all experiences and points of view, the facilitator role is critical. This position usually rotates among the more committed members of the team over time.

The attitudes and goals of a facilitator are usually different from his or her attitudes and goals as a team member. A person may be deeply devoted to prevention work among teens as a regular Faith Partners team member. But when that person serves temporarily as the team facilitator, he or she must set aside individual goals and work to enhance the service and value of the full group, representing a family of services and issues.

The facilitator must believe in the faith institution as a venue of healing and be happy with this individual church, synagogue, or mosque. Experience has demonstrated that a team too often misfires, becomes uncomfortable, or simply fades away when a team's facilitator is angry with the church, critical of its mission, or upset with the current pastor or lay leadership.

It is important for successful facilitators to encourage members to "take charge and take credit" for the service work of the team. The facilitator looks for the possible in all workers, makes sure all parts and views within the congregation are represented and participating, coaches the team toward agreed-upon achievements, and paves the way for team activity with the pastor and other congregational leaders.

Many team members find personal healing in their team's work. But team members should not rely on the Faith Partners Team Ministry for their primary spiritual growth. Team members who use team activity for therapy jeopardize everyone. This is especially true of facilitators.

It is important for a facilitator to have a good working relationship with all of the congregation's leaders engaged in pastoral counseling. When troubled people and families approach their pastor, he or she must have complete confidence in the team's ability to help, as well as an understanding of the ways team can serve. The facilitator helps create and maintain that bond.

Finally, a facilitator must be totally committed to team renewal. A team that does not attract new members each year and engage in new learning and new service throughout the year is a dead team. When every member is focused on the educational and service work of the team, it is the facilitator's job to find ways of attracting new members and recruiting them for this duty.

Talking with the Pastor

Pastors are very busy. They depend on routines they have developed over time to get their work done each week. They usually save their creativity for their sermons and their thinking time for new spiritual growth.

Though pastors will soon recognize that many of the problems identified during pastoral counseling have direct roots in alcohol and other drug problems, they may at first minimize this connection. Often pointing out this connection simply makes them feel like more work is being required of them.

Yet no Faith Partners Team Ministry effort will enjoy consistent success without the full understanding and enthusiastic support of the pastor. To get this partnership, the team must prepare its case carefully and present it forcefully. It is important to plan the first meeting with the view of the pastor in mind. It is also useful to begin by establishing exactly how alcohol and other drug problems exist in the current congregation.

Most business leaders do not know that the majority of people who are addicted to drugs and alcohol are employed – at valuable and critical jobs. Most pastors are unaware that many members (and pastors) experience addiction, and pastors are always surprised at the number of people in recovery from addiction who attend their faith institutions. Having a recovered addict or alcoholic or a family member in recovery involved in early meetings between the team and the pastor is always useful.

The team should assume that the pastor understands and believes in the disease definition of addiction, and they should present the science of addiction in perfect harmony with the faith of spiritual growth. Sometimes, pastors do not believe in the science related to chemical misuse and dependence. This is a real problem and must be dealt with carefully, but persuasively. Present the science of illness along with real facts about the power of healing when medical, emotional, and spiritual issues are addressed. Nelson's book, *Thirst: God and the Alcoholic Experience,* is a valuable resource for pastors on this subject.

There are very good histories within each denomination for positive actions and beliefs toward recovery. Research the issue within your faith. Furnish documents that demonstrate these positive movements and their outcomes.

Explain the process used in the Faith Partners Team Ministry Approach and spell out in detail the working agreement desired between the team and the pastor. This includes showing the pastor the congregational survey, educational materials, and a proposed calendar of events.

Most importantly, listen. When the full story from the team's point of view is presented, carefully note the pastor's comments. From his or her response, determine where there are objections, where there is advice, and where there is enthusiasm. Look for ways to overcome the objections, take the advice, and cement the pastor's ownership and support for the team's work.

Remember that although the relationship with the pastor is critical for success, this relationship is likely to be built on a number of meetings and experiences. In the final analysis, the pastor will trust and work with the team based on actions, not words. So the team must make sure to deliver on its side of the bargain.

As with all sales efforts, it is better to under-promise and over-deliver than the other way around.

Holding an Exploratory Meeting

After weeks of careful preparation, it is time to gather the "willing partners" and see if the ingredients are present for a Faith Partners Team Ministry. The goal of the exploratory meeting is to gather commitments from potential team members and begin the tasks that will define the team's work and goals. At this stage, many people from every part of the congregation will have expressed interest in the project. The exploratory meeting converts this "interest" into "commitment."

Leaders should have realistic expectations. Past experience has demonstrated that approximately one half of those who have expressed an interest actually sign up for duty. There are many reasons for this drop-off. Often, people in early recovery find it is best to make sure they have achieved a stable program of wellness before becoming too active in outreach activities. Others simply have to balance their commitments to voluntary work in the church. Still others will want to "see how it works" before they make a commitment.

It is very important to make clear from the beginning that addiction recovery ministry teams are not the place for people seeking or needing help or counseling with serious personal issues – particularly those related to problems with alcohol and other drugs. People in early recovery do best when they focus on themselves for a time and scale back outside commitments.

Teams need individuals with energy to spare and spiritual, mental, and emotional health to share. The best candidates are people who have been in recovery for some time, those who have special training in the chemical dependency field, and those who have a personal interest in prevention and recovery – often grandparents, teachers, and others with a passion for helping young people with tough decisions.

The first job, then, in preparing for an exploratory meeting is to check the list of people to be invited. Make sure the list has complete information: correctly spelled names, phone numbers, addresses, and the reason the person cares about helping a team ministry. Clergy are a great help in developing this list.

The second job is to determine a date and location for the meeting. Review the needs with the appropriate congregational staff. Visit the available rooms to make sure the seating and other accommodations are appropriate. Make sure the proposed time is not in conflict with other important congregational activities. Make sure the date selected allows three or four weeks for invitations to be sent out, so people can make plans to attend. If possible, make arrangements for coffee or other refreshments at the meeting.

The third job is to promote the meeting. Mailed invitations should go to everyone on the list. A follow-up phone call should be made to everyone one week after the invitations are mailed. Ask the pastor to assist with follow-up calls. Also ask the pastor to make an announcement at every worship service leading up to the meeting. Include an announcement in the printed "bulletin," and post it on the congregation's notice or bulletin board.

Special guests for the meeting should include the pastor, key congregational staff, and members of the congregation's governing body. It is also useful to invite an experienced Faith Partners team member from another congregation. This person may be asked to share the story of another team in formation and the successes and pitfalls of the team's experience.

The fourth job is to prepare materials that will be used in the meeting. In the appendix of this book is the "Introduction to Faith Partners and Team Ministry." It can be reproduced and used as a handout for all of the participants. The second item is the video: People of Faith – Partners In Prevention. Preview this video and make arrangements to show it at the exploratory meeting, giving participants real people - faces and voices representing this ministry.

Estimate the anticipated attendance (half of the prospect list), allow for assured participants (such as the organizers, the pastor, and special guests), and add twenty percent for a safe margin. Using this formula, an exploratory meeting that invites 37 prospective members and has five assured participants should have 28 packages of materials ($19 + 5 + 4 = 28$).

The meeting program should be crafted with as much care as the presentation to the pastor discussed earlier. If the group has (hopefully) already designated a facilitator, this person should lead the meeting. Otherwise, an experienced facilitator should be engaged for the affair.

The meeting must include a combination of presented information, two-way discussion, and an opportunity to "sign up." A typical meeting outline includes:
- Opening and welcome by the pastor.
- Presentation of the Faith Partners concept. (Use "Introduction" handout.)
- Introduce and show the video: "People of Faith-Partners in Prevention."

• Tell stories. (Include outside Faith Partners guest.)
• Review comments and solicit questions.
• Circulate sign-up sheet
• Close in prayer.

After the meeting, call all the participants. In addition, call those who could not make the meeting and see if any want to sign up for service. Report the results of the meeting in letter form to the pastor and leadership. Act on any decisions for work that occurred in the exploratory meeting.

Some action should result from the meeting – even if only one or two people agree to serve this special need. There are many activities a single individual can do within a congregation. Sometimes, it takes more than one exploratory meeting to launch the ministry. Be patient. But stay active and be ready when others are led to join.

With the exploratory meeting, the organizing phase of the team ministry moves to the service phase.

Leadership Training for a Team Ministry

For people who have adopted the vision of a team ministry in their congregation to address alcohol and other drug prevention and recovery possibilities, the prospects are both hopeful and daunting. The thought of starting a new ministry – recruiting people, introducing the idea to the pastor and bringing him/her on board, finding the resources, making a plan and carrying it out – all of this can be overwhelming.

There are decisions to be made about what information to share with others about prevention and recovery. There may be a lack of agreement on the approach to take. How does one prevent alcohol and other drug abuse? Who are the professionals who work in prevention? How effective is it? How does a person intervene with someone who has a problem? How in the world do you get people to go for help? What does it take to recover? Can we solve the alcohol and other drug problem? Where would we start? And would we ever finish?

The questions certainly outnumber the obvious answers. But experience in building Faith Partners teams demonstrates two important paths for beginning and nurturing the team ministry.

First, the mountain can be broken down into hills. What appears to be an impossible job must be seen as a series of very possible tasks.

Second, others have traveled this path. Their mistakes are instructive. Their successes can be replicated.

Volunteers will be reluctant to join any effort unless they can see ways this ministry can help the congregation and ways their contribution will be satisfying to them. Success can be difficult to measure if team members are not clear about what they are trying to do, who they are as a team, what their plan is, and what success looks like for them. Volunteers in a new assignment are often fearful. Training furnishes knowledge, skills, and a process for answering questions and crafting work plans. Equipped with knowledge and skills, the team overcomes their initial fears.

From extensive experiences and pilot projects, the Rush Center of the Johnson Institute has developed proven training programs to equip volunteers in faith institutions with the knowledge and skills required to build effective and fruitful team ministries. The Rush Center's primary work consists of delivering these proven training experiences and operating a full-time service center to share information and promote networking among teams.

Three training opportunities prepare teams to establish ministries that use the Faith Partners Team Approach. They are programmed for different levels and stages of development. Together, they help potential leaders and committed volunteers determine the steps needed to provide an effective and accountable ministry in their particular situation. Through these educational experiences, emerging team leaders learn important information about how other teams have been successful. At the same time, they carefully craft and mold the ministry to fit the specific opportunities of their individual congregation and community.

Introductory Training

Clergy, lay people, and professionals in prevention and treatment interested in a Faith Partners Team Ministry first attend a four-hour introductory session where they are introduced to the "big picture." It begins with a 15-minute video on the Faith Partners story. Participants learn about the role of the faith community in prevention and recovery, research to show the need for such ministry, and the barriers that keep congregations from being involved.

They learn the four basic steps for building an effective congregational team ministry:

1) The exploratory meeting;
2) The congregational survey;
3) The congregational inventory; and
4) The team member selection process.

The goal of the introductory training is to equip participants with adequate information to make an informed decision about initiating a team ministry. A secondary goal is to bring people from the community together so they are aware that others see value in such a ministry and they are not alone in pursuing a way to contribute.

Perhaps the most important aspect of this training is that it offers participants the opportunity to begin the conversation – to begin talking about an issue that rarely gets addressed in congregations though many of the people in the pews are afflicted and affected. The training sessions open doors for talking about different experiences, understandings, and attitudes – differences that have the negative potential of shutting down the conversation. Participants learn about the need to listen to and appreciate others' views, and they learn that judgmental approaches fail, in prevention, and in recovery.

Once someone has attended the introductory training he or she is encouraged to go back to his or her congregation and begin the process of building a team. The recruitment, training, and building of the team ministry precede educational approaches to the congregation. Emerging team members grow through experiences of coming together, working with the pastor, and sharing in the responsibility of starting a new ministry. They reduce fear and hesitancy through action. Teams are urged to take the prescribed steps: learn about the needs and resources of the congregation; recruit a team; and bring that team (3-8 individuals) to the next training offered, the team training.

Team Training

The two-day Team Training is usually conducted in a community or region where several congregations with teams of three to eight people come together to gain the information, skills and resources to initiate, plan, and implement a team ministry in their congregation. A skilled and experienced trainer facilitates the sessions.

Two tracks run through this training, a process track on how to work together effectively, and a content track identifying accurate information to present to the congregation. Team members should to take the time to get acquainted and learn of one another's experiences, expectations, and personal patterns of working with others. The training is interactive, with extensive discussion between team members and among teams. Team members go slowly, build trust, and commit themselves to talking about what their congregation can do – not how they can solve the alcohol or drug problem, but what they can realistically accomplish.

For most congregations, this is a new ministry, one that involves a serious and complex disease, and one that carries a lot of judgment and stigma. There is a direct relationship between how much power and healing a ministry can bring to a congregation and the time and care devoted to building the team. Staying on course and acting purposefully with those relationships can build a fruitful ministry.

Educational Sessions

Team members can replicate the Team Training, three one-hour educational sessions in their own congregation, hopefully at those times when youth and or adults are already in educational settings. Teams title and promote the sessions using language that appeals to general audiences, making it safe for anyone to show up and listen. Team members leave the Team Training with the ability to teach these workshops in their own congregation:

Session One: Prevention Concepts and Strategies

A useful approach to prevention strategies begins with understanding fundamental "risk" and "protective" factors associated with alcohol and other drug misuse and addiction. Risk factors are those circumstances that seem to be associated with higher potential for problems, such as existing addiction in the household. Protective factors are those circumstances that seem to be associated with successful choices and outcomes, such as church attendance.

This training session, titled "What Makes a Difference?" was developed by Roger Svendsen of the Minnesota Institute of Public Health, using research by J. David Hawkins and Richard Catalano of the University of Washington, Search Institute, and the Hazelden Foundation. Participants individually circle the level of risk for fifteen descriptive groups on a handout and then discuss their responses. Examples of the groups are "Young people who work for pay" and "Young people who have friends who use alcohol or drugs."

For example, adults are often surprised to learn that "Young people who say their parents would be upset if they used alcohol" are at the lowest risk for alcohol, tobacco, and other drug use. Parents and other adults routinely underestimate the influence they have over the beliefs and behaviors of young people.

Team members become aware of the importance of "having the conversation." They realize that there is no quick fix or silver bullet, that healthy family behaviors and boundaries will reduce the risk for many potential problems. They begin to trust their own instincts, their own judgments and now have a place where they feel safe talking about these issues. The discussion is rich, eyes are opened, sharing is encouraged, families no longer feel isolated or unsure, and the community is strengthened by this discussion.

Session Two: Six Steps to Share Concern (Early Intervention)

The second one-hour session that can be duplicated in the congregation is a six-step method also developed by Roger Svendsen of the Minnesota Institute of Public Health and based on the earlier work of Johnson Institute. A set of inexpensive videos, titled "See It, Say It," accompanies this approach.

Members of the congregation first discuss how difficult it is to talk with someone about behavior that is disruptive or damaging to relationships without making the person defensive or angry. Why do individuals wait so long to share concern? Why do they watch silently when they see behaviors that worry them? It seems very risky to talk to someone about his or her behavior. Many are afraid they will hurt the individual's feelings or regret what they say. And finally, does it do any good to try to talk to people about negative behavior? After establishing how difficult sharing concern can be, the presentation then moves to a nonjudgmental method of sharing concern by using six steps: I CARE, I SEE, I FEEL, I LISTEN, I WANT, and I WILL.

Step One: I CARE – The first task is to let the person know how much you care about him or her. This starts the conversation in a compassionate way. I love you, our friendship is very important to me, I value the relationship, I care about you – all of these statements let the person know that you are sincerely concerned about him or her. Sharing love and concern has the possibility of opening the person up instead of making him or her defensive. The approach starts the conversation off on the right foot.

Step Two: I SEE – Describe what you actually see. Focus on the behavior, not the person. Do not make judgments or diagnoses. Simply say what you see – "you stumbled on the stairs last night and I smelled alcohol on your breath" instead of "you came in drunk!" Present facts, not impressions. The point of being descriptive is two-fold: The person may be less defensive at the description and the person sharing concern will not regret what he or she says.

Step Three: I FEEL – Emotional ties are powerful and speaking about one's own feelings can help engage the person. This comes from the heart. "I am sad. I am afraid. I am disappointed." These statements let the person know that you care and you have been affected.

Step Four: I LISTEN – It is very important to listen to the person. This is a way to honor and respect the other person. It is a way to acknowledge the serious nature of what has been said. There may be many different types of responses or none at all. Sometimes after coming to this step and finding that the other person is not ready to talk, it may be a good thing to offer to have another conversation at a later time, giving the person ample time to reflect upon what has been said.

Step Five: I WANT – Here is the opportunity to share your perspective, your suggestion about what the person can do to change the behavior.

This is what you want from the person and often it is that you want him or her to talk with a professional about the problem.

Step Six: I WILL – From your own perspective, what do you have to offer? Can you walk with this person as he or she gets help? Can you help the person with a referral? Can you offer to talk about this again or provide support for his or her decision? This is another way to say that you really care.

A 15-minute video, "Calm Down and Follow the Moves," is furnished as part of the training. This video tells the story of two families who demonstrate different ways to express parental concern about tobacco and alcohol use by their teenage children. The video viewing is followed by small group discussion of various situations in which early intervention is needed. The discussion helps individuals find answers to the question, "How do we share concern in a way people can hear us and in a way that we do not regret later?"

The skill that helps people share concern or intervene early is perhaps one of the most empowering skills taught in the Faith Partners Team Ministry Approach. Team members get enthused and empowered when they learn to address hard situations in a more helpful way. They see opportunities to use this skill and understand the need to intervene early. These studies reveal that troubled individuals need multiple intervention statements before they begin to see that they have a problem.

Session Three: Understanding Addiction and Recovery

The third one-hour session taught for replication is a panel presentation. Participants who are in recovery are asked to volunteer to talk about "working the Steps." Panelists answer specific questions after they introduce themselves. The questions are:

• When did you get into recovery?
• To which Twelve Step fellowship do you belong?
• How do you "work" the step (that you are assigned)?
• What role did the faith community have in your life before, during, and after recovery?

Any number of panelists can do this presentation, though it is more interesting to have at least four or five. Each person on the panel uses approximately five minutes for each step, even when each person is covering more than one step at a time. This focused session is extremely helpful in building bridges to understanding Twelve Step recovery. This exercise briefly describes various types of chemical addictions and Twelve Step fellowships. It helps people understand the spiritual nature of these programs. It also helps them examine the role of the church before and after recovery. A great deal of useful information gets conveyed in a very brief time and in a credible manner.

Seeing the faces and hearing the voices of people who have experienced both the pain of addiction and the joy of recovery has a powerful impact. It motivates others in the congregation to share the joy and spread the understanding of recovery.

Participants are very touched by this presentation. The honesty and powerful stories of healing and recovery disarm them. They are amazed at the Twelve Step process and become aware of their misconceptions about it. Because this is such an emotional session, the group is asked to give feedback to the panel, a thanks, a statement of their own, an insight, and/or how they have been impacted by this presentation. It is also a time to teach about anonymity and confidentiality.

A useful fifteen-minute extension of this session is to ask team members to respond with healing stories of their own. The leader can say, "We have heard powerful stories of healing and recovery. We now have a better idea of the experience, strength, and hope that these individuals bring to our team. What healing experiences do the rest of us have to share? What gifts do we bring? It may not be an experience of recovery and that is okay. What can each of us contribute in our own unique way?"

This exercise builds the bridge between team members in recovery and those who are not. It encourages personal commitment and responsibility.

Along with team-building exercises during the team training, teams are also given the assignment to craft initial planning for their individual team strategies and programs. Though training time is limited, teams are urged to consider several next steps and report back to the larger group. They are asked to address these questions:

- What is our mission? our vision?
- How do we share responsibility for identifying community resources?
- By what method can we educate ourselves initially and the congregation eventually?
- How can we begin to plan at least three annual events: youth education; parent and other adult education; and an emphasis on recovery for the whole congregation, preferably during a worship service?

The training concludes with teams making even more specific plans: When and where do we meet? What are our individual assignments? Next steps?

Skills Training

From six to nine months after the Team Training, team members are ready for a day of skills training. The goal of this training is to take the teams to the next level by providing more advanced information, skills, and resources they need to sustain, strengthen, and expand their ministry. Individually, team members need an opportunity to clarify once more the purpose of this ministry and then identify and affirm their own contributions with a renewed sense of commitment.

This training includes inspirational speakers, an update on the ministry across the country, opportunities for sharing and support, and workshops on areas of interest. This exchange of information is done through speakers, panel presentations, small group discussion, and interactive workshops.

Workshops are offered on the basis of need. They include but are not limited to:
- Improving team facilitation skills;
- Preparing for a recovery worship service;
- Developing youth prevention strategies and activities;
- Planning parent and other adult education sessions;

• Working with community resources;

• Researching how families are affected by addiction; and,

• Examining other addictions.

The skills training is an annual training in regions where there are active team ministries, providing an opportunity to renew, refresh, and equip team members and teams on a regular basis.

The Process of Building and Sustaining a Team Ministry

A good way to understand the evolution of the team's ministry within the congregation is to visualize the team as the family member who has just gone to Al-Anon. The person has just discovered how much he or she has been affected by addiction. The person wants to teach others everything he or she is learning. The person wants to tell others what to do. There is something they can do – and it has to do with changing their own belief systems and their behaviors, not someone else's. It has to do with talking about this issue differently.

The individual learns that the way one handles this issue within a family will have an impact on the person with the disease. The individual begins to see what he or she can do. So it is true with the team – its members begin to visualize the effective role they can play. They realize that they can't fix all of the people with alcohol and other drug addiction, but they can take some significant steps by changing their own attitudes and behaviors.

The team can begin to speak aloud of addiction by using facts and research, not myths and misunderstandings. They can interpret and promote understanding the Twelve Step process of addressing addictions. They can be witnesses to the healing of addictions by sharing their own stories. They can provide a consistent, loving and nonjudgmental presence, and if there are family members who are ready or even alcoholics or addicts who are ready for help they can guide them to the community resources.

Once team members talk about prevention, intervention, and recovery, they can begin to determine how this information might be integrated into the life of the congregation, through religious education classes, through presentations to groups, and through seasons of awareness involving testimonies and literature.

Seven
Preparing for Team Service

Mature team ministries take many forms and serve in ways that meet the specific needs and opportunities of the individual congregations. Teams can make the task easier, however, by beginning the ministry using the tools that have proven successful. This chapter outlines procedures and projects that help a team to identify specific needs and opportunities and to create a history for team work that will nurture the group through the building process and for years of service in the future.

The foundation work of a new Faith Partners Team Ministry should include these tasks:
- Survey the congregation.
- Conduct a congregational inventory.
- Set up team operations.
- Recruit team members.
- Research community resources.

Surveying the Congregation

Much is made in disciplines of spiritual growth about the difference between "talking the talk" and "walking the walk." In the final analysis, of course, it is the "walk" that counts. Yet any seasoned minister will agree that it is important not to ignore the "talk." Knowing how people think or feel not only helps one understand how they act, it also gives clues on why they might act differently than they think or feel.

Survey research is a tool that measures "talking" and "walking," allowing leaders to make good decisions in their work. This tool is extremely useful in establishing team ministries for several reasons.

First, people often fail to disclose their personal experiences with addiction disease or the risks for disease that exist in their families. Society's negative attitudes toward addiction foster shame and stigma for parents and siblings as well as for alcoholics and addicts. And most have found it easier to keep these secrets to themselves – even in the safety of the congregation of their faith.

Second, false information abounds about every phase of misuse and dependence on chemicals. Many congregations have not resolved the ambivalence associated with "normal" use of alcohol, let alone accepted the science that demonstrates how certain individuals have a unique propensity to become addicted. Myths about drinking rituals, chemical reactions, loss of control, enabling behaviors, and use of "will power" color every conversation and decision about alcohol and other drug consumption, behaviors, and problems.

Third, because of secrets and myths, leaders often fail to discern either the nature of the problem within a group or the opportunities for service and success. This is true in businesses, the military, schools, and government, as well as institutions of worship and faith. An earlier participant in the Faith Partners Team Ministry Approach was a Texas Episcopal priest who did not believe his congregation would be at all interested in a team ministry. He held this opinion even though he was himself a recovered alcoholic with more than 20 years of successful recovery.

He was shocked to learn that his relatively small congregation of 100-150 members included 18 people in recovery from alcohol and other drug addiction and more than 50 families who had experienced addiction within their families.

Because successful surveys are useful tools, survey research has become a proven science. The recommended Faith Partners Congregation Survey tool has been developed professionally to help determine the potential for a team ministry in any congregation. The questions in the survey have been used countless times with thousands of congregational members. The findings have local meanings when reviewed as a local survey. They also can be measured against the history of similar surveys throughout America and over the span of many years of survey experience.

For these reasons, it is important to (a) use the survey as it has been constructed, (b) introduce and conduct the survey in the manner recommended, and (c) submit the survey results to the Faith Partners Service Center for analysis.

It is recommended that the pastor and team facilitator both participate in announcing the survey at a regular worship service of the congregation. Many congregations repeat this survey every few years, usually in connection with a sermon on the power and possibility of addiction recovery. Here are six reasons why teams have found the survey a rich and vital part of their ministry.

1. A survey yields information about the impact of alcohol and other drug use and misuse on the congregation.
2. It provides data about how members view the possibility of the congregation being involved in a ministry of recovery and prevention.
3. It provides another way to find volunteers who want to help in the ministry.
4. The results will help the team focus on areas of greatest need in the congregation. This information will be used later, when the team writes its action plan.
5. Surveys also serve as educational tools, particularly for those members who deny that addiction is an issue for the congregation. (Survey results typically show that one of every five respondents has been concerned or personally affected by someone else's misuse of alcohol or drugs at some time in his or her life.)
6. Finally, and perhaps most important, surveys mandate and legitimatize the team's work.

Discuss the details of the survey project thoroughly with the pastor. Plan the distribution of the survey form. The forms can be distributed to the congregation during the introductory remarks at the primary worship service, and then explained and collected at the end of the service. Or the worship leader can ask everyone to remain seated after the service, during which time the survey may be distributed, explained and then collected as people leave. Either way, the best results occur when the survey is done during the regular worship service.

A less efficient and effective method is for one or two committee members to visit various meetings, classes, choirs, and circles of the congregation, explaining the survey and distributing survey forms. This system is more time-consuming and produces a smaller rate of return. This, in turn, reduces the accuracy of the survey.

Maintaining the integrity of the completed documents is essential. Collect all the completed forms. Do not review or destroy any survey form that is collected. Do not tabulate or review the forms. Send them by insured mail to:

The Rush Center of Johnson Institute, Faith Partners Service Center, 2525 Wallingwood Drive, Building 8, Suite 804, Austin, Texas 78746.

Conducting a Congregational Inventory

The purpose of conducting a Congregational Inventory is to find out what resources and opportunities are available in the congregation and will be useful to a team ministry directed at problems with alcohol and other drug misuse. These include tangible things, such as bulletin boards, meeting facilities, newsletters, and literature racks, as well as intangible things, such as youth groups, men's groups, women's groups, study classes, social activities, and Twelve Step meetings.

Another important purpose of the inventory is as the first collaborative work project for team members. In addition to gathering important information, the team members are carrying the idea of the team ministry to all aspects of the full congregational ministry.

The information gathered should be as precise as possible, detailing the contact person (with phone numbers) for each activity, the deadlines for newsletters, and other essential information.

Team ministry is more successful if activities are integrated into the existing life of the congregation rather than staged as "stand alone" functions. The inventory provides the information that makes such integrated service happen.

Conducting the inventory is also a learning experience for the facilitator. Research can be divided up. Small teams of two can be assigned to gather the information. Volunteers skilled in writing can reduce the inventory to a report. At the conclusion of the inventory, the report should be shared with the pastor and become the topic for discussion by the full team.

Setting Up Team Operations

The congregational survey and inventory are not only key elements of beginning a team ministry, they can be useful projects to keep the ministry on course and connected to the full congregation. In many teams, these events are part of a cycle of tasks the team will perform each year. The cycle includes:

- Recruitment drive;
- Team development;
- Education program;
- Service and referral program;
- Team promotion; and
- Evaluation.

Team subcommittees will often work on these various elements, but as a group the ministry will generally work through these phases of activity each year. The team's governance and operations must take this cycle of activity into account. Most teams operate on a consensual basis, meeting regularly to review projects, make group decisions, acknowledge successes, and assign new tasks.

The team meetings should be regular, with members knowing the full year in advance that they occur on specific dates (e.g., second and fourth Wednesdays of the month) at the same time and place. Established teams can often do their work in a monthly meeting, with time devoted to business, program reports, and team education. Most beginning teams need meetings every week, or every other week. Some teams meet as a Sunday School class or Wednesday night study group.

A recommended meeting format includes:

- Spiritual growth. This usually takes the form of an opening prayer and/or meditation, closing prayers, and prayer request. A nurturing and centering activity can be built around a book chosen for its spiritual and service content from which the team reads individually a chapter each month. An event at each meeting, then, is a ten-minute comment time on the chapter reading for the month.
- Community building. Members should share experiences of personal growth and service related to the team ministry involvement.
- Mission management and oversight. This involves a review of the year's service plan, hearing reports on individual projects, selecting and assigning team members for roles and projects, reporting specific requests made to the team, and handling other team business.

Some teams prefer to operate on a committee model, managing business in sessions separate from the reflective and team building activities. However the team conducts its affairs, it is essential that everyone feel comfortable with the process and that the rituals of the team ministry become more meaningful with time and practice.

The role of the facilitator is key to the development and conduct of the team's business. The facilitator is part quarterback and part coach, making sure that the group succeeds in becoming a team and in reaching its goals. A good facilitator forgoes authoritarian leadership for a style that is participatory, drawing out the insight, experience, motivation, and intelligence of each team member. This style fosters a feeling of power and purpose owned by each and all members of the team.

The responsibilities of the facilitator include:

- Preparing meeting agendas and leading the group through them.
- Acknowledging everyone's contributions and making sure all members have an opportunity to speak.

- Communicating regularly with the pastor. This should take place in a regularly scheduled meeting, not in happenstance encounters.
- Creating an environment in which every member feels accepted, cared for, and valued.
- Asking questions, encouraging discussion, and promoting problem solving. Making sure all aspects of an issue or problem have surfaced before resolutions are crafted.
- Noting and celebrating success.
- Making sure meetings do not get bogged down in detail and that they begin and end on time.

In addition to determining the frequency and time of regular meetings, and the format of these meetings, the team should discuss and decide who can conduct certain roles and what are the broad goals of the team for the year. Most teams designate a secretary for maintaining the team roster and taking notes at the team meetings.

The team should have an annual process for goal development and a monthly process to making sure the goals are being met. At the same time, the team needs to adopt guiding principles for its actions and visit these principles on a regular basis.

Through discussion, the team should craft a system for responding to requests for help and tracking referrals that are made by team service contacts.

Recruiting Team Members

The survey and inventory projects are usually conducted by a few people who want to start a Faith Partners Team Ministry and have secured the support of the pastor and church leadership. These two projects make the full congregation aware of the possibility of service. Many members of the congregation will have questions about the idea and may consider participating if they get more complete information.

To take advantage of this opportunity, the organizing team should begin its recruitment effort immediately after the survey. As was discussed earlier, it is important to include people with recovery experience, people trained as professionals in the chemical dependency field, and congregation members with special interest in young people. The steps of a recruitment effort include identifying prospects, making personal invitations to service on the team, and integrating new recruits into the team effort.

Teams often look for prospects outside of the traditional leadership of the congregation. Many people concerned with chemical dependency who have stayed in the background can be very motivated by this issue. To build the prospect list, start with people who expressed interest during the survey or who attended the first exploratory meeting.

Talk to the pastor, members of the governing board, study group teachers, and others in leadership, asking them for referrals and recommendations. Ask them to make calls. Using the congregational inventory, visit and attend various congregational functions and activities that reach the full congregation. Focusing on events that attract parents can be useful.

Post notices on bulletin boards and in congregational newsletters. In addition to advancing the team's recruitment needs, this is a good opportunity to explain the team's mission to the full congregation.

Ideal team members are naturally caring, emotionally stable, willing to keep commitments, and trustworthy. Team members engaged in referral service must be able to keep confidences. People should not join the team in order to deal with a current family crisis.

While recruitment is an ongoing feature of team activity, a specific "drive" to recruit new members should occur each year. Many teams schedule a worship service annually that includes a sermon on addiction, a personal testimony of recovery, a survey, and an appeal for new members.

Researching Community Resources

Addiction to chemicals is a progressive disease, beginning with early experimentation and, too often, advancing to institutionalization, jail time, and even death. A lot of damage to individuals and property occurs, in situations of too much drinking or drugging – even when addiction or dependency is not involved.

As was discussed earlier in this book, symptoms occur at every stage of problematic chemical use and addiction. It is society's habit, however, to overlook symptoms in earlier stages of the illness. The task of the team ministry is to find appropriate resources to address symptoms for every stage. Communities offer a range of resources, generally including:

- Voluntary recovery support organizations. These include, but are not limited to, Alcoholics Anonymous, Narcotics Anonymous, Al-Anon, and Nar-Anon.
- Voluntary associations committed to education about alcohol and other drug addiction, recovery, and appropriate public policies. These include local chapters of the National Council on Alcoholism and Drug Dependence, the National Association for Children of Alcoholics, and others. Check the websites of these groups for local contacts. Local prevention agencies can be found by viewing www.jointogether.org or www.cadca.org.
- Addiction treatment facilities. These may be residential or out-patient. They may honor private health insurance, be funded by tax dollars, or require cash payment.
- alcohol and other drug addiction counseling services. These include private practice counselors, services included in broader health care clinics, and counselors in public agencies.
- Prevention agencies. These services include a broad range of educational and activity experiences designed to prepare young people for the decisions about risky behaviors. Some are school based. Others available for individual needs.
- Mental health agencies. Private and public mental health care providers are more and more aware of addiction issues, particularly when people have both emotional difficulties and a propensity to misuse or depend on alcohol or drugs.
- General health agencies. Hospitals, clinics, public health centers, and individual doctor practices have long ignored addiction issues, but are beginning to understand the relationship between general health and alcohol/drug consumption.

• Youth centers. Recreational and educational facilities devoted to young people, including Boy's and Girl's Clubs, often have services directed toward individuals with problems or those at risk for addiction.

The primary job for the congregational team is to compile a directory of resources that are useful to the membership. Secondly, the team's goal is to establish relationships with these services so that referrals can be appropriate and timely. Collecting the information for this directory is a useful team project that stimulates learning as well as relationships among team members.

From resource lists gained from the telephone directory, contacts in the recovery community, and team members engaged professionally in the community, visits can be scheduled for team members. Working in pairs, team members can visit each facility, using a standard questionnaire. These reports are then gathered and compiled into a full directory.

The directory can also include the names and telephone numbers of team members, key principles and goals of the team ministry, and some basic information about the disease of addiction and its symptoms. This directory becomes a key service element when distributed to the congregation.

Another benefit of the visitation effort is to identify experts in the community who value the work of congregational ministries and can attend team educational events and arrange other project features helpful to the team ministry.

The visitation effort will produce information about community-wide meetings, events, and resources that the team may want to pursue. It is a good idea to have team members report on visits to the full team at regular meetings to prompt discussions and suggest outreach options that may help meet goals.

Crafting a Mission and Plan

As the team completes each phase of organizational work, many in the congregation will see positive effects. The work will have included assembling the team, researching the needs and assets of the congregation, and inviting members of the congregation to participate in its learning. This process of lighting a candle, will have generated a power of attraction.

Teams may be tempted to focus this new energy and rush the good news of recovery to every member of the faith community – "installing" the enlightened viewpoint into waiting hearts. Long-term success, however, results from careful planning and prudent program development. Providing an addiction recovery ministry is something a team does for and with – not to – its congregation.

That's why successful teams craft mission statements and action plans for their service work. Armed with the survey information, team members who have prepared themselves for service stop and create a plan to follow. The team usually sets aside a special meeting, even a retreat, to review the needs, set reasonable goals, and choose workable programs. The action plan process has three parts – each requiring the best thinking of the group in making important decisions:

1. What is the team's purpose? (Where do we want to go?)
2. What results will satisfy that purpose? (How will we know when we are there?)
3. What actions will produce those results? (Will a train, plane, bus or car best get us there?)

Purpose, results, and actions seldom work together without planning. Taking the time to craft and fit these pieces together is a wise team investment.

A statement of purpose, or mission statement, is usually one sentence that conveys the values that bring the team together and the broad intentions of its work. It reminds members why they were called together. It sets the sights, as well as boundaries, of its ministry. Finally, it tells people outside the team what need is being served and how.

With some quality time and a skilled facilitator, the group should be able to convey its purpose with clarity and passion in very few words. This statement should wear well with time, posted on the doorway to action as long as the team serves.

The statement of goals can be more expansive, and it will change with time to match the conditions within the congregation. Here are some typical goals:

- We want parents in our congregation to know how to talk with their children about drugs and alcohol.
- We want the helping hand of recovery available to any congregational member who suffers with any stage or involvement with chemical misuse or dependency.
- We want members to realize the family nature of addiction illness.
- We want an open relationship in our congregation with Twelve Step fellowships.
- We want our team to be visible and available to support anyone facing trouble with addictions.
- We want recovering people to feel safe sharing their experiences.
- We want young people to have the knowledge and skills to make wise choices about alcohol and other drug use.

Most congregations cherish any and all of these goals, or results. The immediate task of the teams is to make priorities that match the need evident in the survey. This process is much like the Twelve Step process for challenging defects of character. There is usually no question about the fact that most people suffer from all known defects of character. The job is to address the ones "between you and your next drink." The team should select goals that most quickly and substantively will (a) help the most people, (b) demonstrate the value of the team to the congregation, and (c) build a foundation for further work that addresses current and future goals.

There is no need to reinvent the wheel when it comes to actions that achieve goals. Activity suggestions, plans, and options are available from a wide variety of organizations. Organizations devoted specifically to the prevention and treatment of alcohol and other drug problems are available in books, magazines, newsletters, and on a number of websites. These activities divide naturally into three types: educational activities, support activities, and help-response activities.

Educational activities include distribution of literature, conducting classes or events, sponsoring individuals to attend outside training, and field trips to places of interest. Information can be directed at congregational members generally, or to certain groups, such as Sunday School teachers and youth. Information is often inserted in other activities, such as lessons within another class or a booth at an event. Ideas, formats, and supplies for educational activities are readily available through many prevention and recovery organizations.

Support activities use association with others as a tool to enhance personal or spiritual growth. A lot of healing occurs when people with similar issues or views associate together. Such gatherings include retreats, trips to ball games, picnics, and volunteer teams taking meals to homeless shelters. Visits to open Twelve Step meetings, and other Faith Partners Teams and events related to addiction prevention and recovery are excellent support activities.

Help-response activities make direct assistance and referral services available to members of the congregation in specific need. Most often, this happens when someone asks for help as the result of pastoral counseling and the pastor asks the Faith Partners Team to help. Depending on the pre-arranged system, the pastor will give the individual the name and number of a team member willing to provide direct help. Or the pastor may arrange a meeting between a team member and the individual requesting help.

Exactly how and what kinds of direct help can be available needs to be discussed between the team and the pastor. These arrangements usually begin at an introductory level and grow as the team grows and as the pastor gains confidence in the team and the system. Frequent adjustments are normal. The advice and participation of team members who have themselves recovered from addiction is essential.

A beginning point in designing team activities, selecting priority projects, and matching them to the results list and team statement of purpose is a general brainstorming session. Here again, the role of the facilitator is critical. Proposed goals can be posted on easels or the wall. Then activity or project suggestions can be written on large "post-it" notes. Members of the group can post, discuss, and exchange activity suggestions on each goal sheet, arriving at group consensus for near-term and long-term priorities.

The opportunities for bridge building within a congregation, and outward to the community, are never ending in a vibrant congregation. People, issues, and circumstances all change, like the shifting images within a kaleidoscope, awaiting creative, persistent, and motivated responses by an effective team ministry.

Eight
Pastors as Coaches

A current movement in health care views the patient as a fully participating member of the "treatment team." The movement's goal is to significantly alter the traditional view that sick people present their maladies and ailments to skilled medical doctors who use their superior knowledge and experience to diagnose the illness and prescribe the appropriate cure. Seeing the professional as the "fixer" of health problems is now considered a narrow view in the pursuit of wellness.

This new paradigm acknowledges the patient's knowledge and experience with his or her own body as well as the patient's power and responsibility to enhance wellness. Seeing the doctor and patient as partners in good health advances wellness. People with a large stake in their care not only heal quicker, but they also engage in wellness practices that prevent further illness.

Consumer advocates in the mental health field advance this philosophy with the slogan: "Nothing about us without us."

Congregations in Partnership

The partnership between clergy and worshipers to effect spiritual healing and growth is a more established practice. To a greater or lesser degree, every traditional worship model engages the individual on a path of spiritual growth. Pastors provide the instruction, coaching, and encouragement for this journey through activities that range from sermons and individual counseling to bedside visitations in times of crisis. But the individual takes primary responsibility for the success of his or her spiritual journey.

The Faith Partners Team Ministry Approach is built upon this idea of partnership. A team ministry has three parts: the pastor, those team members who accept special training and responsibility in addiction recovery issues, and the entire membership who benefit from new understanding and ready, appropriate responses to alcohol and other drug problems. As a result of the Faith Partners Team Ministry, the congregation as a total unit encourages conversations about use of alcohol and other drugs, symptoms of addiction, and choices facing young people about the use of tobacco, alcohol, and drugs. In addition, the congregation welcomes and supports individuals and families who have survived their addiction experiences and enjoy enriched spiritual lives as a result.

The congregation discovers that honoring recovery is a practical way to celebrate God's mission and purpose.

Reservations

Congregations, like society, often harbor deep reservations about engaging in service to people experiencing addiction. Many approve and engage in "missionary" tasks to assist the helpless, homeless, and addicted in their community. But this work is often seen as an outreach to "lost" people. Admitting that all people are "broken" to some degree and that the potential for chemical dependence is universal (even including clergy) is another matter. Engaging in a ministry that addresses everyone's propensity for illness and everyone's opportunity for wellness takes both vision and a measure of courage.

Pastors often have reservations about a team ministry devoted to addiction recovery. This chapter address shares four of the most frequent reservations, then disclose information about a recent meeting in which twelve core competencies in chemical dependency were developed and recommended for clergy by an inter-faith panel of leading American clerics.

The first reservation about the Faith Partners Team Ministry Approach experienced by pastors is the practical concern about time and costs. The modern faith institution is a multi-faceted service organization with major plant investments, growing program needs, and increasing financial pressures. Pastors who entered the ministry for the challenge of learning and teaching spiritual growth are understandably distressed at the significant time required for financial reporting, staff leadership, program planning, and facilities management.

In practical terms, pastors engaged in Faith Partners Team Ministries find that this ministry does not put more paper on their desk. By providing enriched team resources, it actually moves action from the pastor's desk to the team. National surveys of veteran pastors report that more than 55 percent of the counseling issues presented have roots in issues related to misuse and dependence on alcohol and other drugs. Through a Faith Partners Team, pastors have a network of trained and experienced assistants right in the congregation. By opening dialogue between congregational peers, healing is facilitated and the ministerial opportunity is shared.

The costs for this ministry are reasonable. They include training and materials to support team members. The major investment is the experience, passion, and talent of team members – furnished at no cost to the congregation as a personal "giving back" for the grace that has worked in their lives.

A second reservation is concern that the congregation has neither the need, or the desire to engage in such a ministry. Many pastors can see and understand the general need for team ministries devoted to alcohol and other drug addiction, but they might not see that need in "my congregation." This view, of course, assumes that the pastor has a deep and thorough knowledge of his or her "flock." They are often shocked and dismayed to find the degree to which people hide issues and concerns related to alcohol and other drugs.

People afflicted and affected by misuse and dependence of chemicals learn early to avoid connections between drinking and drugging and the consequences that emerge. People who consider themselves paragons of honesty regularly lie to doctors, employers, and pastors about drinking and drugging. For family members, this covering up of the evidences and side stepping of consequences is seen as both a help to the troubled person as well as defense against consequences for the family.

So it is not unusual for pastors to be surprised at either the depth of the problem in the congregation or the willingness of members to participate in a solution.

The third reservation is the fact that clergy training seldom includes information about alcohol and other drug problems or practices useful to address these problems in pastoral counseling. Of America 185 certified seminaries of every faith, less than 20 provide pastoral counseling courses on addiction and recovery.

In national surveys of clergy engaged in pastoral counseling, most pastors report that they are not very well equipped to deal with addiction issues. A study of clergy conducted by Columbia University's National Center on Addiction and Substance Abuse reported that while 92 percent saw the importance of having knowledge of addiction, only 12 percent had received any seminary or post-seminary instruction in the disease, its symptoms, or recovery.

Specific knowledge development is no small matter. The growing scientific knowledge of addiction demonstrates its genetic and biological basis, while authenticating the success of spiritual paths of recovery. Restoring this bridge between science and faith is not a haphazard endeavor. Successful pastors, particularly those engaged in pastoral counseling, profit from specific training. Fortunately, training opportunities are growing, both in seminaries and in post-seminary programs.

The most successful Faith Partners Team Ministries have resulted when pastors and the team leaders attend and complete training together. The Team Training offers fundamentals in the nexus of faith and science that are often a stepping stone to further study and instruction.

The fourth reservation is the most serious. And that is the reluctance to move beyond the judgmental view of addicted people that society has held onto for many centuries. Successful ministries have overcome the traditional belief that punishment is a required element in dealing with a chronic illness like addiction.

The most prevalent use of the punitive view is that alcohol and other drug addiction can be "prevented" with youth-directed education featuring harmful consequences of chemical use and misuse. The messages that people who engage in such activity are "bad," "wrong," or "sinful" have not worked. Increasing the criminality of chemical use has likewise failed as a preventative measure. America's drive to expunge from society the consequences of addiction has resulted in loosely marking people as "criminals" to be hidden from sight through the jail-building spree of the 1990s.

This approach, in addition to failing, is difficult to square with core faith philosophies of respect for human life, belief in a loving Providence, and the power of spiritual healing. Nevertheless, congregations often reflect the fears of society more than the potential for healing. In this regard, Faith Partners Team Ministries represent a "road less traveled." Witnessing the miracle of recovery first hand, however, presents ample reward.

A wide range of experience is authenticating the healing approach over the punitive approach. Treatment practices that featured "hot seats" and "breaking down" people with programmed guilt trips have proven not only useless, but harmful to successful treatment and recovery. New therapeutic technologies, such as Motivational Interviewing, which rely on respect for the client and partnership in the treatment, are proving powerful. The classic peer-to-peer, non-judgmental precepts of Alcoholics Anonymous are gaining more and more credibility with each scientific review.

To place this trend in a spiritual context, it can be said that God's message from the beginning is that His love is more powerful than the judgment of all humanity. There are two parts to this message. First, that speaking to the value and potential of every human being is the most effective pathway to the heart. In AA, this is called the "power of attraction." The second message is that passing judgement on others is most often the work of people, not God, though God's name is often invoked in the process.

Legacy of Concern

Many efforts to address alcohol and other drug addiction within institutions of faith have occurred over time. Church action and leaders largely drove the temperance experience in America. Regarded in retrospect as a misguided attempt to control public behavior, the experience discouraged religious organizations from advocating public policy positions for many years. Yet the desire to help members with difficulties remains an interest and concern for many.

This interest is reflected in a long list of articles and books in every denomination devoted to alcoholism and paths of faith useful to recovery. Some denominations support special organizations with a focus on addiction awareness and appropriate responses, such as the Recovery Ministries of the Episcopal Church or the Presbyterian Network on Alcohol and Other Drugs.

A number of residential treatment centers for addiction originated as recovery facilities for priests and ministers. Some ministers with recovery experiences, such as Father Joseph Martin, became leaders in the addiction recovery field. Father Martin's "Chalk Talk on Alcoholism," originally commissioned for a U.S. Navy treatment program, is still a standard educational tool.

Vernon Johnson, an Episcopal priest in Minneapolis, was encouraged by his bishop to start a church study group following his treatment and recovery from alcoholism. The study group developed the technology of "intervention" and became the Johnson Institute.

Together with the National Association for Children of Alcoholics, another pioneer movement devoted to the family aspect of addiction illness, the Johnson Institute convened leading clerics from every recognized faith organization in America in 2001 and 2003. The purpose was to develop strategies to better prepare pastors for counseling people afflicted and affected by alcohol and other drug use.

Known as the Clergy Training Project, these two panels assembled ministers, priests, rabbis, imams and other pastoral ministers with significant experience in religious training and knowledge of addiction and recovery. A key product of their deliberation was the "Core Competencies for Clergy and Other Pastoral Ministers In Addressing Alcohol and Drug Dependence and the Impact on Family Members." In effect, the "core competencies" attempted to provide a general framework for what should be expected of every candidate for ordination.

The unanimity achieved across the faith traditions of Catholics, Protestants, Jews, Muslims, and Native Americans was astonishing. In their report, the 31 panel members enumerated the primary roles in building and maintaining pastoral relationships as

• To comfort and support individuals.

• To create communities of mutual caring within congregations.

• To educate the congregation, and sometimes the larger community, about issues of importance to people's well being.

In their report, they found that "each role offers particular opportunities to address the subject of alcohol and other drug dependence and its impact on individuals and families, and each opportunity requires a particular set of knowledge and skills." (These "core competencies" are included in the Appendix.)

The findings of the panel engaged in the Clergy Training Project are reinforced by the experience of the Faith Partners Team Ministry Approach. A congregational team ministry requires the understanding, leadership, and support of the pastor. A pastor's success in building a caring congregation and serving the congregation's specific needs is enhanced by partnership with a congregational team devoted to chemical health at every stage of personal development.

Nine

A Team Ministry Case Study: Faith Partners in Action

The Faith Partners Approach, team ministries dedicated to prevention and appropriate responses to alcohol and other drug problems, currently serves in more than 100 congregations in Minnesota, Texas, Oklahoma and Ohio. Their experience is the basis for this book. Here is the story of an individual team ministry in rural Minnesota. Names are pseudonyms.

The Reluctant Leader

Like many stories of innovation, this one started with one person's desire. She was in her sixties, a writer, mother of three grown children, and a long-time friend of Bill W. She had moved to this small river town a number of years ago. Her drinking days were far behind and most of her current friends knew her only in sobriety.

One Saturday morning at her regular Alcoholics Anonymous (AA) meeting, she decided to throw out an idea she had been sitting on for some time. She shared her desire to develop a recovery ministry in her own congregation – an average-sized Lutheran Church in southeastern Minnesota. She described how alcoholism had ravaged her family and herself. She spoke of how her spiritual journey through the Twelve Step program had led her back to her faith in God and how she wanted to help open that door for others.

The thought of connecting her recovery life to her faith life was received with mixed responses. Some thought it was an idea long overdue, while others reflected on their negative experiences with organized religion and doubted her idea would work. Though discouraged by the discussion, she had planted a seed.

A few months later she learned about Faith Partners, an organization dedicated to equip congregations for addiction prevention and recovery through team ministry. A new member of her congregation, also in recovery, had learned of her interest and told her about the team ministry approach. Though this information rekindled her passion, she had become engaged in several writing projects and felt her energies were too limited to pursue the idea. She also held some doubts from the earlier discussion in her AA group. But she now knew she was not alone in her desire and reluctantly committed to talking with the senior pastor.

She discovered that the pastor's family had been touched by alcoholism. He was more than receptive to the team ministry idea and pledged his support and help, provided that the leadership remained with the members. The door to this ministry swung open and a new team ministry was on the way. The writer who started the ball rolling decided to jump on for the ride, but she was clear she did not want to lead the ministry. She determined her contributions would be to write articles for the newsletter or bulletin and help keep the team on track by keeping meeting notes. Her true leadership revealed itself at the first team event: a Celebrate Recovery Worship Service.

The team decided a recovery story was essential to the first worship service to celebrate addiction recovery. They discussed getting a "hired gun" (a person in recovery experienced in telling their story) from outside their community. They also discussed having the team members give their testimony in the worship service.

Two issues dominated the discussion. First, was there a danger that an outside speaker would only emphasize that while addiction is a problem, it doesn't exist in "our" church? Second, were there any team members willing to share this part of their lives to church members who were unaware of their addiction history? What would people do with this new information? In the end, the team decided that the primary message to give their fellow members was that alcoholism is a problem and it exists within the church – possibly including a member of the congregation sitting right next to them.

Finally, Sarah, the writer with the original idea, volunteered to give her testimony. But she had serious reservations. "I have been a member of this congregation for a number of years and still don't feel comfortable," she said. "But I am willing to share my story as long as it is okay with my husband." Her husband gave her two thumbs up, and he was the proudest person in the congregation on Recovery Sunday.

During the week before the special service, she shared her story with the pastor. This deepened their relationship and helped him link his sermon to her message.

The night before, she got cold feet and called her recovery sponsor to express her fears. The sponsor calmly responded, "Imagine you are talking to one other woman and that your message is for the individual still hurting." That morning, she communicated a clear, caring message.

At a Monday night AA meeting, a woman approached Sarah, looked her in the eye, and said; "I heard you on Sunday morning and knew I needed to be here." The newcomer was met with tears of joy and a rush of excitement. The whole team sensed God's presence in this event and believed a giant step had been achieved in creating a safe, caring environment to talk about addiction in the faith community. The whole team knew that moment they had made the right choice to have Sarah speak.

The experience was empowering for Sarah. She decided that if she could take the basement ministry to the sanctuary, she could also take this basement ministry to the community. Her excitement spilled over to the rest of the team as she led another project: an open meeting with a potluck supper. "Feed them and they will come," was her motto. Her hope was to create an understanding of how following the Twelve Steps helps an individual grow along spiritual lines. The event helped demystify the Twelve Step program, and it encouraged others to integrate their faith and recovery lives.

Interested community members packed the room to hear stories from team members in recovery and to enjoy good food and fellowship. Team members not in recovery discovered how powerful the stories were and how the principles of AA mirrored messages from the Bible.

With Sarah's desire and leadership the team had experience, traction, and a growing passion. She would later help lead the team in its second year by becoming the co-facilitator.

The Prodigal Son

He was married without children and had grown up in the community, but he had moved away for a number of years. He had returned to the place of his childhood and recently realized he had been suffering from the disease of alcoholism. John attended the exploratory meeting for an addictions ministry at the invitation of the senior pastor. He was kind, unassuming, and soft-spoken. When the participants were asked to introduce themselves and their reasons for coming, he volunteered to be first. His voice shook as he described his struggle with alcoholism. You could hear a pin drop. He was nervous, but more importantly he was genuine and sincere. He expressed the need for the church to respond to people like him without judgment, but with dignity and grace.

His story set the tone for the rest of the meeting as he and the rest of the participants realized they were not alone. As others shared their own "brokenness" from addiction disease – either personally or as a family member, the room seemed to get a little smaller as the team felt an immediate rapport and closeness. Others who had not experienced alcoholism in their immediate families expressed a desire to respond to those in need or to focus on prevention for the sake of children. The goals of this ministry were described and the group was offered an opportunity to participate in training to equip them to do this ministry. Eleven of the thirteen decided to take the next step and committed to attending the team training. John was one of them.

The night before the training, John called to back out. He was questioning his recovery and doubting his ability to contribute. He described the importance of his church involvement in his recovery and wanted to participate, but he was unsure about how the rest of his team would respond to his struggles. He was given three choices: not joining the ministry team, joining later when he felt stronger in his recovery, or growing with the team while participating from behind the scenes. He decided to continue participating, with the understanding he needed to focus his energy on his recovery and to separate his recovery from his involvement with this ministry. The ministry team was a safe and supportive place, but it was not his primary place for healing. He was also asked to continue to be honest with the group about his struggles. The team embraced him from the start and accepted his struggles with respect and grace.

Like the rest of the team, he attacked the first tasks highly motivated – filled with gratitude and wanting to give back. This became easier as individuals gravitated to the tasks that best matched their personalities. John and another team member took it upon themselves to develop a resource list – a contact directory of support services in the community dedicated to addiction prevention and recovery. They wanted a directory much more useful than the yellow pages. Their goal was that when the person in need reached out, the hand that reaches back would be credible and responsive, to insure a positive experience from the start. They used their own experiences and personal research to develop an extremely useful tool.

John continued to struggle with his recovery, having difficulty with the principles of AA. Following his directory project, he needed time to concentrate on his healing. After the first year he decided to step away from the team ministry to focus his energies on understanding his disease and working out his recovery solution. The team respected his decisions all the way through the process and was disappointed to see him step away. He continues to stay in touch and helps from behind the scenes whenever asked.

The Wounded Healer

Recently divorced and with two young children, she was feeling the sting of her situation. As she walked through the doors of the church she loved, she felt the stigmas associated with being a single mother and being divorced from someone still practicing his alcoholism. This hurt her deeply, but she realized most of the cold stares and glances with accompanying whispers were not malicious. Most individuals simply did not know how to respond to someone they truly did love and cherish. Her experience of discomfort and distance helped kindle the passion to create a healing climate she desired, one others could use in their own brokenness.

Too often, people survive difficult experiences only to harden their hearts and harbor bitterness. Joan was different. Her experiences, however difficult, gave her a heart of understanding. Even in the midst of pain and confusion, she recognized her need for wholeness, and she reached out to others. Her ministry took many forms, including working with children to create an environment of acceptance and openness. She lived the true essence of prevention – one person taking an interest in another's life.

This tenderness also revealed itself when she invited her ex-husband to attend the team's first recovery worship service and the related adult education hour. The adult-education speaker talked about the spirituality of recovery. More than 75 people attended from the congregation, the Twelve Step fellowships, and the community. Some who attended had never graced the doors of this church or possibly any other. The speaker had them laughing and crying with his family stories and in the process educated all in attendance, making it a little easier to talk about addiction. One person who had received a special invitation followed the speaker to his car wanting to know more. All it took was an invitation.

Joan understood the pain family members experience in the throes of this disease. Most of the early inquiries received by the team ministry came from family members. She worked through the team to provide a useful response for the hurting family member. She and another team member founded an Al-Anon meeting in the church. It started with just the two of them sitting across from each other. It slowly grew to twelve core members with over twenty attending most meetings. The members report a richness in the meeting in which people are receiving support and healing.

The Servant Leader

This congregation was truly home to Joe. He grew up in the area and had a successful life raising four children. He spent a lot of time in the service to the congregation and was one who loved the Lord. After many years as a member and a number of congregational assignments he became a Stephens Minister, a lay ministerial position. It was through his experience with a Stephens Ministry care receiver that he was first introduced to the symptoms of alcoholism. He felt ill-equipped to give this person care—beyond prayer and sharing spiritual fellowship with him.

As a result of this and other experiences, he found himself sitting in the exploratory meeting for this new team ministry with twelve other congregational members, including two other Stephens Ministers. He was committed to learn more about addiction and through his experience with this care receiver discovered a heart for the alcoholic and others affected by addiction disease. He rarely missed a team meeting and became a strong team member, serving in any way possible from setting up a room for a presentation to attending regional Faith Partners Network meetings representing the team.

His unswerving attitude of living each day in God's grace and joy was always a breath of fresh air. His attitude was consistent with those in recovery. He really wanted to make the team successful and served in many ways to make the effort an experience for the entire congregation. The team learned that a person didn't have to be in recovery to be a part of this ministry and found his Biblical perspective refreshing and stimulating.

———

These four team members and many others during the first year of growth found that their first and foremost challenge was to face their personal doubts, fears, and uncertainties, often based on years of silence and guarded interactions with the church. As is often experienced in the recovery healing process, a natural transformation takes place inside one's skin about being public with the conversation of addiction – either illness or recovery. It is not uncommon for those who get involved in this ministry to have been touched by alcohol and other drug abuse. But the same reluctance to discuss problems and solutions out in the open is shared by most volunteers. At first, most team members want to stay in the security of the shadows, where it may feel lonely but also safe.

As the team formed, learned, and served, members began to feel that this ministry gave them a sense of belonging and purpose. Often, they felt called by God – integrating their lives as children of God. They saw the focus of their service to the congregation and community as providing prevention messages during life transitions, equipping individuals to share concern with each other, and providing a safe, caring environment in which the addicted can experience hope and healing.

Gathering the Team

With the full support of the pastor and a passionate team leader, the next step was to gather a team. The congregation's official invitation was an announcement of a new ministry to help people prevent and recover from addictions. The message described a team ministry and offered special training for volunteers who responded. The positive support of the pastor was crucial to the announcement. But just as welcome and important was his list of individuals he thought would be interested in the project. He personally invited them to an exploratory meeting, describing the ministry and encouraging their participation.

The best candidates turned out to be people who have been in recovery for some time, have special training in the chemical dependency field, or have a personal interest in prevention, such as parents, or grandparents. The team leadership soon discovered the power of providing choice on the one hand with a level of screening on the other. It seemed many of the team members felt called by God as a way to give back for the miracle of their own recovery. As a result, this distinctive ministry gained members new to congregational service of any kind. They had found their niche.

The congregational survey triggered the next wave of volunteers. Providing a rapid information flow for new volunteers proved essential to keep their interest during the organizing phase. Requests to new volunteers had to be very specific. Many new volunteers wanted to fulfill individual assignments but did not want to attend meetings. The early activity list for volunteers included teaching a class, monitoring a table at the ministry fair, sharing their testimony, talking to the church staff, and setting up for an event.

Unpacking Team Stories

Like passengers on a train, the team discovered that members come on board at different stations or points of time. They also played various roles on the journey. It was vital, however, that they agreed on the direction the train was headed. A successful team rides on two "rails." One rail is relationship building. The other rail is service to the congregation. The successful team balances the work between these two rails. Leaning too heavily in either direction can cause the train to derail and the ministry to fail.

Learning about one another provided a useful starting point for building team relationships. The stories revealed each member's interest, experience, and passion. The team devoted meeting time to "unpacking stories." Through this activity, members experienced transparency and vulnerability that led to trust, confidence, and healing. They found as they began to understand one another's stories they were better able to help one another turn their weaknesses into strengths. As "wounded healers," they offered their experience, strength, and hope as a source of healing for members of the team, and ultimately for the community.

Honoring the Passion

Early on, it became clear that the Faith Partners Team structure and formal connection to the congregation was vital for success. Just as apparent, however, was that individual passion for the ministry was the fuel for action and achievement. Although connecting to the structure is important to the life of this ministry, the passion of each team member drove this ministry. The team's leadership soon understood that their purpose was to recognize the gifts and passion of each member and guide that energy into purposeful ministry.

Soon, this passion was manifested through new AA and Al-Anon meetings in the church, education and prevention activities, the development of a resource list, new books in the church library, newsletter articles, and many other activities. This passion is usually the result of life experiences. For example, Joan brought experiences of conflict with police in the handling of her alcoholic brother. She shared that she often witnessed the police disrespecting him. Her response to these experiences was to stimulate a group vision of community education and collaboration. The team organized an event, drawing community leaders, police, attorneys, judges, clergy, medical professionals, and people in recovery. The event was an opportunity for leaders and professionals to hear recovery stories and to learn that they hold important tools to assist recovery. Building on Joan's passion, the team found that the plan dovetailed with the pastor's hope to go beyond the four walls of the church and minister to the larger community.

A mother's experience with her son's addiction and its consequences also illustrates mobilizing passion. Her feelings of helplessness and hopelessness fostered her desire to assist other parents, so they would not have to face the same difficulty she experienced navigating the community's different systems. Another mother resonated with this idea and together they started a parent advocacy support group. The first meeting featured a presentation by a detective. He described the community drug scene, provided pictures of drug use paraphernalia, and listed signs for parents to observe.

Passion energizes action. By unpacking team member's stories, recognizing their passion, and guiding energies into meaningful ministries that meet the needs of the congregation and community, the team grows and gives.

Remaining Faithful

The original team included a number of recovering people who were sprinters. They wanted immediate results. They had great energy for the short-term but tended to disappear if things didn't happen fast enough. Team ministries need both visible activities and consistent presence over time. Frequently the number and size of activities are used to measure success because it is natural to recognize the high energy required to organize a specific event or project, and it is harder to measure the work and patience necessary for a long-term ministry.

Mother Teresa was once asked, "After all these years, do you feel you have been successful in your work?" Her response was, "I didn't start this work to be successful, but to remain faithful to my calling."

The team's facilitator helped the team focus on the long term "calling" of the group: increasing knowledge throughout the congregation, encouraging open conversation about alcohol and other drug problems, and building a long-range service ministry. The group found that this ministry needs the energy of the sprinter, but it also needs the stamina of the marathoner. One role of the facilitator was to keep the ministry moving forward, utilizing whoever was on the train. Sometimes this meant gently reminding team members to keep participating in team meetings. The facilitator found that the more a volunteer's passion was sparked, the more they showed up. After eighteen months, ten of the twelve original members of the team were still active in this ministry.

The Faith Partners experience indicated that finding the balance between short-term success and long-term viability is an individual team discovery.

Celebrating team faithfulness to the mission and recognizing the consistent work of the individual team members was the consistent contribution of the facilitator. She acknowledged short-term and long-term progress at every meeting. As a result, the team never lost sight of the prize, recognizing the accomplishment of individuals as well as those of the team.

Engaging the Congregational Leadership

After a series of successful experiences, the team began to consider the importance of becoming sustainable over time. It became clear that engaging the congregational leadership early and often was a vital key to long-term sustainability. The team collaborated with key church staff at critical times, such as event planning, recruitment, church council meetings, and the annual meeting, building lines of communication and good working relationships.

The first and most important relationship continued to be with the senior pastor. The pastor's approval paved the way for support from the governing board. The team was thrilled when the pastor attended the Faith Partners introductory training. He immediately understood the potential for a ministry to those families affected by alcoholism and other addiction. He reported that approximately one-third of congregational members had been negatively impacted by addiction. He saw from the start this ministry was not just for this church, but for the whole community. He has been an incredible advocate – opening the doors to the congregation, its leadership, and the community.

The team members have also built solid relationships with key church staff and leaders, including the youth director, the coordinator of Stephens Ministry coordinator, the Adult Education chairperson, the children's ministry, and the parish nurse. These staff and lay leaders have become advocates of the team's work.

The youth director arranged special presentations, recruited youth for the team, and facilitated discussions for a faith-based prevention curriculum. The children's ministry coordinator invited the team to present a program on coping with the transition to middle school for fifth graders. The parish nurse attended Faith Partners training and made referrals to team members. And the Stephens Ministry coordinator embraced this ministry as complimentary to, rather than competitive with, her ministry.

Understanding the Congregation

Looking at earlier experiences with the Faith Partners Team Ministry Approach, the team discovered that many congregations failed because they didn't find out the will and receptiveness of their individual faith community. Other teams struggled when they researched the congregation's interests but chose not to plan their activities around the perceived need.

This team wanted to know this information – and act on it. They did not want to feel as if they were grasping at straws. The suggested Faith Partners Congregational Survey helped to gauge interest, quantify need, build support, and recruit volunteers. The pastor announced the survey from the pulpit and the newly recruited team collected the surveys, starting the process of putting a face on this congregational ministry. Although the sample size was small, those who answered were clearly receptive to team ministry. The results of the first congregational survey were:

- 75% favored reaching out to suffering addicts;
- 89% favored providing parent prevention strategies;
- 80% favored providing youth prevention activities;
- 72% favored providing programs to help spouses; and
- 79% favored providing space for recovery programs.

Sarah, John, Joan, Joe and all the other team members felt extremely validated in the team work when they reviewed the findings. The survey created a clear mandate and legitimized the work of this team. It also furnished a prospect list of new advocates willing to help promote programs, assist in providing adult and youth educational opportunities, and attend the programs that were offered. The team immediately laid plans for periodic congregational surveys to continue tracking feedback for the team's direction.

Setting the Tone

Following the basic team training, the team felt a keen awareness that they were part of a "movement" that unites, equips, and supports congregations so that they can make a difference in the lives of individuals and the community. The team also understood they would not get many chances with this ministry. They had learned in training that investing time and thought in the initial tone the team set was critical to the success of this ministry for years to come.

The cornerstone for setting the tone was the mission statement. The team's first meetings were spent crafting such a statement. Key words emerged in their discussions, words like *acceptance, forgiveness, nonjudgmental, confidentiality, and caring*. The majority of the team had experienced finding their faith through Twelve Step programs.

They named the effort:

"Pathfinders: a ministry where faith and recovery come together for people affected by addiction."

Their mission was to provide a safe, nonjudgmental environment within their church in which people could discuss and understand alcoholism, other addictions, and the prevention of alcohol and other drug abuse. The primary goal was to create a public discussion in the faith community, instead of a conspiracy of silence. The hope was to provide a safe, nonjudgmental environment for those experiencing the disease of alcohol or other addictions where they could feel comfortable seeking help and through this ministry be guided to the help they needed.

The team carefully assessed three dynamics that would help guide the goals in this important ministry. The first was the overall mission of the church and how the team would integrate its work into the life of the congregation. The second was following the congregation's lead by listening and responding to the congregational survey. And the last was exploring how the many gifts, talents, and passions of the team members would drive this train.

The team goals were then listed:

- Organize regular educational programs for youth and adults for the understanding and prevention of alcohol and other drug misuse or abuse;
- Equip family units (spouses, adults, and young people) with knowledge, skills, and resources for the prevention of alcohol and other drug abuse and other addictions;
- Sponsor an annual Celebrate Recovery Worship Service;
- Provide a safe, welcoming atmosphere for recovery through offering Twelve Step Programs, such as Alcoholics Anonymous, Al-Anon, and Alateen groups;

- Inform congregational members through written materials on current local, confidential recovery resources; and
- Work with local churches and other community groups to inform and educate the community on prevention and recovery.

Welcoming the Conversation

"We have never taken time to discuss our beliefs about alcohol and other drug use," the chair of the congregation's Adult Education Council said. As a mother of two teenagers, she and her family attended a Teen Improvisational Theater (IMPROV) performance sponsored by the Pathfinders Team. The performance centered on underage drinking and parental involvement in the prevention of alcohol and other drug misuse. With the help of the youth director, the team prepared the IMPROV troupe with real situations from the community to use in their scenes. More than 125 middle and high school students, parents, and interested adults attended.

"After the presentation at church, the doors were open for any conversation," the mother and church leader said. Later, she told a team member how the IMPROV program stimulated more discussion at their home. Other parents and families echoed this sentiment. The event had opened the door for discussions in a number of families and for other adult education presentations.

This experience underscored the lessons that the team had learned in team training, including that permission to discuss openly alcohol and other drugs, without automatic judgments, is the hallmark of a healthy and healing congregation. They remembered a saying from Twelve Step fellowships that "we are only as sick as our secrets." A climate of "permission" to share one's hurts, whether physical, emotional or spiritual, is not an automatic endowment of religion. It must be cultivated and nurtured on a regular basis, they discovered.

The second major growth event for the Pathfinders Team was to plan and present their first Celebrate Recovery Worship Service. The plan was for two young people in recovery from alcoholism to tell their stories and answer questions with the senior-high youth group. Then, two family members were scheduled to describe their experience living with someone suffering from alcoholism to a confirmation class of middle school students. The plan called for the Sunday elementary school staff to teach a related lesson that Sunday.

With the full cooperation of the congregation's staff, the team planned the liturgy, music, sermon, testimony, gospel readings, and the adult education hour.

The team wanted the congregation to know that people in recovery have a life worth celebrating and that they can be powerful witnesses to those who are still struggling, even those in denial. The message was to combat the shame that traps those in the throes of their addiction. They called for persons of every age to experience the blessing and celebration that is diametrically opposed to the shame, despair, and fear that empower stigma. The power of shame is its secrecy, they said. When a person is open and accepted, shame melts.

Following the special worship service devoted to the team's message, there was a commissioning of the team members. After the services, many congregational members made good use of the resource table, where printed information on addiction prevention and treatment was available. Of course, many members avoided eye contact with team members, or left by another door. But team enthusiasm was high.

They knew the conversation had been started.

Special Rewards

A number of events fell into place for this ministry to succeed. An individual or group of individuals had a vision and passion for this ministry. The congregational leadership was willing to take the risk. Team members made time for training. And the congregation was receptive to the possibilities.

Sarah and the others in recovery found ways to bring the advantages of Twelve Step spirituality into the life of a congregation without stripping it of its worship tradition and modes of fellowship. Working together, everyone found the special reward in establishing the congregation as a place that blesses recovery.

Another team member in addiction recovery said: "For me, serving on the Pathfinders Team brought my recovery full circle. My life is finally integrated, Sunday through Saturday. I can be open about my recovery, and I can be actively involved in a congregation, serving and being served."

Nurturing Change:
Help For People In Difficulty

A favorite story told in recovery circles demonstrates the limitations of a narrow point of view.

A flood was rapidly filling the valley. People were warned to leave their homes and drive to safety. Joe, an earnest believer in Providence, insisted on staying in his home, watching his property, and praying for delivery. He believed the threat was a challenge to his faith, and he was determined to keep his trust in God at any cost.

A Sheriff's Deputy came up the driveway, spreading the warning and urging Joe to leave. Joe sent him away, saying God would demonstrate his power over nature. But the flood waters began to rise, and soon the driveway was completely covered.

In a few hours, the water rose to cover the fence posts in the yard, the well over the cistern, and the steps to the front door. Most of the people in the valley had fled. State Troopers worked in fishing boats with small outboard motors to continue the search and offer rescue to people threatened by the flood. Yet Joe resisted, turning the boat away and staunchly calling on God for protection.

Eventually, Joe was forced to scramble to the roof as water filled the house. A National Guard rescue helicopter spotted him and dropped a rope ladder to the roof. Now filled with fear, but defiant in his position, Joe angrily threw the rope ladder back to the helicopter. "My God is stronger than any flood," he said.

Later that night, Joe drowned.

Facing his creator, Joe pouted, "Why did you let me down?"

"What do you mean, I let you down," God replied. "I sent the Sheriff, State Troopers, and the National Guard. What else do you need?"

Many well-meaning religious leaders are slow to realize that science and medicine are within the realm of the spiritual when it comes to overcoming addiction. Experience in recovery has demonstrated in the last 60 years a nexus of science and faith not only is desirable for recovery and an enhanced life on this earth, but is likely part of a Providential scheme. It is helpful to realize that few of God's creatures arrive in advanced stages of spiritual fulfillment. All of us experience stages of change but do so in different ways.

The co-founders of Alcoholics Anonymous themselves experienced "spiritual awakenings" in dramatically different forms. Bill Wilson reported the sudden experience – a "great white light" in his hospital room, accompanied by a new clarity and fresh insight. Dr. Bob Smith reported the "educational variety" of spiritual awakening, gaining insight and perspective a step at a time. Studies have shown, however, that no matter how people change their addictive behavior, most follow a fairly standard process.

Work in the 1980s by psychologists James Prochaska and Carlo DiClemente identified six "stages of change." They placed these stages on a wheel-shaped chart. According to their research, individuals are seldom aware that their behavior is somehow related to their failure to achieve personal goals and ambitions (though others, such as friends, parents, co-workers, are very aware). They cannot even contemplate change and certainly lack readiness to advance to any new state of understanding or changed behavior.

Therefore, the first stage in the change cycle is "pre-contemplation." Circumstances or coaching either force or entice the individual to advance. But this advancement in readiness has further phases. Once people think about finding a new way to reach personal satisfactions, they find themselves on the wheel itself and begin five passages toward behavior change. These five stages are:

- Contemplation – Considering that some kind of change might lead to different results.
- Determination – Making a decision to do something different, even a small thing.
- Action – Actually following through on the decision, taking a step out of the ordinary and toward a hope or vision of different results.
- Maintenance – Assimilating the new action into daily life. Adapting a new life style may be incremental, but the new behavior becomes a normal behavior with intensive focus or special concentration.
- Relapse – Losing concentration on the new action when focus is still required. Falling back into the comfortable groove where results are known, even though negative.

One goes around this wheel once or many times before stepping off the merry-go-round into a permanent behavior change. The essential lesson for coaches observing this process is to meet and engage the individual "where they are" – emotionally, intellectually and physically. Whether the coach is a parent, friend, pastor, sponsor, or professional, it does little good to address "action" or "maintenance" issues when the individual is in "contemplation" or "relapse" stages of change.

Meeting people "where they are" is a significant attribute of peer-to-peer mutual help practiced in Twelve Step Programs. Veterans, of two weeks or twenty years, engage newcomers on the basis of their common experience. They sit side-by-side in meetings, each attending to his or her own healing.

Lessons learned from studying this "wheel of change" have driven major advances in counseling techniques and recovery support practices. The most popular strategy for using "stages of change" with troubled individuals and families "where they are" is known as "motivational interviewing," or "motivational enhancement." First developed in the addiction recovery field, the practices are now widely used in mental health practice and general pastoral counseling.

In their classic text, *Motivational Interviewing* (1992), William Miller and Stephen Rollnick identified five basic principles for this practice. They are outlined here because they illustrate successful practices advanced by faith team ministries at the individual, congregational, and community level. As has been stated repeatedly in this book, we believe addiction illness cascades from individual, to family, to community, to society. Recovery also heals in this cascading fashion, and the principles of motivational enhancement are useful in both observing as well as supporting this healing.

The principles are stated from the viewpoint of the "coach":

1. Express empathy.
2. Develop discrepancy.
3. Avoid argumentation.
4. Roll with resistance.
5. Support efficacy.

These engagements occur at each stage of change. They provide useful assistance while acknowledging that "coaches cannot score points." The individual must take responsibility for change, but coaches can move the conversation along, challenge weak thinking, and provide important reinforcement. Counselors who work from this "coaching" perspective develop sophisticated skills using these basic principles.

Successful pastoral counselors who nurture spiritual growth will recognize the logic and usefulness of these principles from their experiences. The principles can be learned and used by coaches at any level and stage of experience. All that is required is a caring heart, an open mind, and the ability to engage people non-judgmentally as equal objects of God's love. These notes, then, are not exhaustive or even thorough examinations of the principles. We share a taste of each concept in the hope it will inspire more study and use.

<u>Express empathy.</u> The critical component is an attitude of acceptance on the part of the coach. It is not required to accept behaviors or outcomes. But it is essential to accept people–without reservation and without judgment–and to allow them to accept themselves. For some, this may simply mean adopting an attitude of "there, but for the grace, go I." For others, more effort is needed to identify with the individual in need or trouble. Finding a common experience or belief is essential to building

rapport. Empathy by definition is genuine. It cannot be conjured, worn or practiced. Saints Francis and Clare of Assisi engaged the lepers as themselves, adopting the core meaning of "compassion" – to "suffer with."

Develop discrepancy. Accepting people for who they are does not extend to helping them stay in turmoil or difficulty. People contemplate change when they perceive that their current behavior fails to take them to personal benefits or goals. Third parties, or coaches, are very useful in helping people register the difference between their actions and their dreams. People seldom discern discrepancies through inventories by spouses, parents, or friends. But issues raised by third parties register deeply, even if not acknowledged at the moment.

Avoid Argumentation. Argument immediately changes the subject from "what is right" to "who is right." People addicted to alcohol or other drugs always win the argument, because they cannot be wrong in their own eyes. Avoiding this trap is the hallmark of a successful coach. Good coaching does not ignore the evidence that people often make choices that are not in their best interest. But the coach avoids the temptation to apply a diagnosis, or label, to the person. The experience of Alcoholics Anonymous is telling: stay out of the business of diagnosis. Bill Wilson wrote: "We do not like to pronounce any individual as alcoholic, but you can quickly diagnose yourself." A good coach never answers or engages a defensive or argumentative statement. As Miller says, "resistance is a signal to change strategies."

Roll with Resistance. If challenges start arguments, and arguments don't work, what does a coach do? The best answer is to keep the conversation going until the individual comes to better conclusions. This philosophy is at heart of Jesus' "resist not evil" message. "Turning the cheek" is not a tactic of defeat. It is a tactic of defusing the language and emotional straitjacket of confrontation. It denies victory to the power of fear. Rolling with resistance lets people fire their fear-driven weapons, but watches them land in unexpected and non-threatening places. It is here that constructive listening becomes the most valued tool of the coach. It is here that the troubled individual finds the resources for change and healing are at hand. This self-discovery powers change in ways no lecture can.

Support Self-Efficacy. Without hope, there can be no change – no victory. People with healthy emotional lives know they are responsible for their well being and that they have the tools to adjust what they do in order to reach where they want to go. People with an impaired vision of themselves still have the tools for change. They just don't know or believe it. Self-efficacy is restored when they discover (or re-discover) their power and responsibility to seek change and find new pathways of progress.

Addiction has physical manifestations. It is a brain disease that "hijacks" our ability to think or make choices. Nonetheless, such "powerlessness" does not prevent taking responsibility for change. This traditional Alcoholics Anonymous message is confirmed in countless studies of counseling practice. Unlike the traditional health issues in which the patient presents a problem to a professional for "fixing," addiction calls forth the individual's power and responsibility to "fix" himself or herself.

Reinforcing this idea is a useful and responsible task of coaching. At each "stage of change," people in difficulty tend to voice their fears, hopes, and conclusions. By reinforcing the insights that perceive reality and suggest new actions, coaches build self-confidence and help the person regain self-efficacy.

––––––––––––––

Nothing in the above discussion is meant to prepare the reader to do professional counseling, or to suggest a program of action for someone in crisis or in advanced stages of alcohol or other drug addiction. People with significant withdrawal symptoms and other signs of advanced addiction need professional health assistance for detoxification and specialized treatment and rehabilitation.

However, the core philosophies of modern treatment and recovery flow from the material in this chapter. Even though people isolate themselves more and more as addiction illness advances, literally hundreds of conversations occur that are usually ignored. By broadening the understanding of addiction throughout a congregation and learning these underlying principles of coaching, Faith Partner Teams are able to promote emotional health and spiritual growth. In many cases, troubled individuals aim toward recovery long before reaching critical health stages. In many more cases, families and others affected by addiction disease avoid their own deterioration by understanding the stages of illness and the tools of change.

Successful Faith Partners Team Ministries promote understanding and skills. They also link the congregation to appropriate professional resources for individuals in critical stages of illness that are ready for change. Everyone in the congregation learns a greater appreciation for the power of faith and hope.

Eleven
Nurturing Change for Everyone

The failure to adequately address addiction problems until they are in crisis stage contributes to the fact that addiction to alcohol and other drugs is one of America's leading health problems. Alcoholism ranks third, behind tobacco addiction and obesity, in premature deaths. The systematic delay in addressing symptoms of addiction assure three costly results:

(a) People begin treatment very advanced in their illness.

(b) They require the most expensive remedies.

(c) They have a reduced chance of attaining full recovery.

It is not too much to say that the traditional addiction treatment response in America is stuck. While multiple responses are becoming more and more available, society still views addiction in terms of street-corner drunks and addicts who exist at the margins of society and need to be removed still further by either treatment or jail.

Similarly, the traditional prevention response to problems with alcohol and other drugs is also stuck. Prevention programs are vital to the management of all health threats.

America's attempt to prevent the onset of addiction in individuals is a study in political correctness, rather than measured effectiveness. For starters, government sponsored prevention efforts are discouraged, and in some cases prohibited, from mentioning alcohol consumption, misuse or addiction. For instance, the legislation authorizing the President's Office of National Drug Control Policy specifically confines the office's fiscal authority to issues of illicit drugs, not to include alcohol consumption by adults. Even though society's costs from alcoholism are more than six times the costs of illicit drug use, every major effort is directed at illegal drugs.

More useful are efforts to identify "risk and protective factors" related to early use and misuse of mood-altering chemicals by children and adolescents. Observing that young people with certain experiences and protections are at less risk than others to develop crisis difficulties with drug and alcohol consumption, an industry of prevention has grown up around ideas to enforce these protections and circumstances. Millions of public and private dollars are dedicated to the idea that society can protect or police its way around addiction disease.

Risk factors are undeniably true. For instance:

- Children who delay experimentation in use of alcohol and other drugs are at a lower risk to develop dependency.
- Reduced access to alcohol reduces consumption.
- Young people who have friends who drink and drug are more likely to also drink and drug.
- Young people who work for pay are more at risk for early use of alcohol and other drugs.
- Children who spend multiple evenings away from home are at risk for drug and alcohol problems.
- Children who attend church are less likely to drink or have alcohol problems.
- Young people who talk to their parents regularly about alcohol and other drugs are less likely to become chemically dependent.

At the same time, programs designed to reproduce these protective factors have been disappointing at best. Trying to keep drugs out of the country, prohibiting access to alcohol, presenting the negative consequences of drinking and drugging, generating "alternative" activities for spare time, and controlling environments are all standard (and very expensive) strategies that have not recorded significant changes in behavior over time.

This does not mean, of course, that Faith Partners Team Ministries should not pay any attention to these risk and protective factors. Rather, these ministries can and do note these risk and protective factors. The factors, however, are approached in a more holistic framework, which produces more effective changes in attitudes and behaviors.

Faith Partners Teams have three perspectives essential for healing. They are appropriate when considering healing for individuals, neighborhoods, nations, or society.

First, appropriate responses to addiction illness should be available for any and all stages of interest, curiosity, and difficulty, from prevention to full recovery.

Second, everyone has a stake in prevention and conquering this illness, no matter whom or when it strikes.

Third, wellness is more likely to develop through timely and consistent programs of love and service than through authority-driven programs of judgment and control.

Behind these three perspectives is a conscious effort to undermine and remove the "us-them" thinking that drives so much of the traditional response to alcohol and other drug difficulties. This is the strongest asset of faith settings in dealing with stigmatized illnesses – whether addiction, AIDS, or obesity. The faith approach is inclusive – we are all subject to the human condition. Everyone demonstrates his or her "brokenness" in different ways. Within the congregation, people continue to address one another in a loving connectedness that disallows anyone to leave the table.

This principle is at direct odds with the principle of addiction. One of the strongest symptoms of addiction is isolation. As people fall under the control of mind-altering chemicals, they choose to be separate – they burn bridges. In their denial, the central plea is to be "left alone."

In the last chapter, we dealt with the concepts and practices that lead troubled people out of this isolation and separateness. What does the congregation do to prevent individuals from beginning the journey that leads to trouble with drugs and alcohol?

Before going to the answer to that important question, let's address the "us-them" tendency. People learn early to think about people with problems as "them." "We" don't have a problem. "They" have a problem. It is human nature to feel superior, to mark people as different from ourselves, and to separate into groups: good or bad, native or foreigner, graduate or dropout, sanctified or sinner. It is also wrong. It is wrong because it doesn't square with doctrines of any faith. And it is wrong because it doesn't work. Alienating people hurts both parties: the hated and the hater. Chopping off segments of society as "less than," "defective," or "hopeless" costs everyone, spiritually, economically, and socially. Feeding the hungry, healing the sick, and nurturing the helpless are the tasks of the healthy faith congregation.

The chopping, unfortunately, does not stop with the defective. Society also condemns the recovered, keeping them at a distance, hiding their powerful stories, and denying their rightful place at the table. The clearest example of this is the near universal practice of people in recovery attending Alcoholics Anonymous and Al-Anon meetings in church basements far from the congregations where they attend to their religious practice. It was noted earlier how pastors are shocked to discover both the prevalence of addiction illness and addiction recovery in their congregations.

Faith Partners Teams reach out to everyone, and a wonderful synergy develops. Who better to power and lead the congregation in awareness and prevention efforts than the members who have felt the pain and worked for recovery from chemical misuse and dependence? Why not journey together in an on-going congregational experience of physical health, emotional wellness, and spiritual growth?

Few people take the work of making children aware and competent about making choices more seriously than people in recovery. They know with some certainty that their own children are very likely prospects to have alcohol and other drug problems.

The Faith Partners Ministry then, does not "target" people at risk. They address everyone in the congregation. Faith Partners Teams listen as much as they teach. Faith Partners Teams honor recovery and provide appropriate service opportunities for people who have experienced recovery. Faith Partners Teams link every phase of awareness, intervention, treatment, and recovery to opportunities for personal and spiritual growth.

To understand how these more positive approaches to conversation, teaching, and healing can lower risks for chemical dependence – for children and adults – it is helpful to review the four phases of chemical use that lead to chemical dependence. Like many chronic diseases, including cancer, emphysema, and diabetes, addiction develops over time, presenting a variety of symptoms during each development phase.

For chemical dependency, these phases include:

1. Learning the Mood Swing: Discovering the feelings delivered by chemical use.

2. Seeking the Mood Swing: Beginning a regular use of chemicals in order to change feelings.

3. Harmful Dependence: Getting drunk or high increasing in importance. Experiencing less and less control over decisions to use.

4. Using to Feel Normal: Using is required to "feel normal." The goal of regular use is to avoid physical or psychological discomfort.

These phases are more fully developed in *Good Intentions, Bad Results*, a Johnson Institute publication by Carol Remboldt. The congregational team comes to understand that these stages are progressive, becoming a spiral into addiction if unchecked. Crossing into the fourth stage, the individual experiences loss of control. The brain has been "hijacked," to use the phrase of a key government researcher. The drugs do the decision-making. Family, friends, and associates who wait for this stage to act on their concern have usually waited too long. Faith Partners Teams with members drawn from a cross-section of the entire congregation understand the signs of enabling and neglect. With experience and training, they demonstrate the power of a spiritually committed group to love and attend to the growth of all.

The training that builds and maintains this congregational network is covered elsewhere. The broad elements of proven prevention strategies are presented here. The first six are developed from findings and experiences reported by the Federal Government's Center for Substance Abuse Prevention. The last two are unique to faith enterprises. These elements were originally aimed at prevention for children and adolescents. The principles are universal, however, and are expressed here for individuals of any age who are making choices about the Mood Swing.

Here are the fundamental prevention elements:

1. Talk.

People stay connected to one another through conversation. Listening to small children chatter is a vital responsibility and task of parenthood. We get release from frustration and resentments by sharing them with others – even strangers. It is said in recovery circles "we are only as sick as our secrets." We often describe Twelve Step groups as "talk therapy."

When young people get silent, their troubles grow. Parents are advised to always keep good communication with their children, especially when it is difficult. Caring congregations do likewise. One form of service to others is to be a "greeter" at worship or other spiritual services. Simply being at the door, and giving each entering person a look in the eye, a smile, and a hearty welcome does wonders for the greeter and the greeted.

2. Involve everyone.

It makes a tremendous difference when parents and other adults get involved in their children's lives. Each experience builds a memory. Too often, when young people "act out," they are ignored or activities are changed or cancelled. Troubled adults are also left to go their own way. It is just easier and calmer to let people go their own way. But if that person is nurturing resentment, bad feelings, or simply wants to concentrate on artificial mood changers, leaving him or her alone simply advances the difficulties and, more often than not, the illness.

Staying involved and maintaining positive activities are worthwhile services to others. This does not mean encouraging someone's bad attitude or compulsions. Reflect a positive light toward others by greeting them even when they are sullen or aloof. Nurture relationships by carrying through with ballgames, shopping, or social activities. However, be careful not to feed ridiculous behavior or cater to outrageous demands.

Congregations are about fellowship, shared activities, and mutual concern. This on-going involvement is good friendship, good service, and good prevention.

3. Set limits.

A parent's clear, sensible rules for behavior are a vital and stabilizing force in a child's life. These rules should be consistent and enforced. Limits on adult behavior are also essential. Unacceptable behavior should be challenged. Give friendship, conversation, and reasonable help. Don't let people trample your personal limits.

Al-Anon practices and principles are helpful in establishing personal limits and maintaining detached love and concern.

4. Be a power of attraction.

Children need role models. Adults need examples of faith-centered living. Maturing social skills, making appropriate choices, and dealing with daily stress are all taught through example. Do not take part in unhealthy or dangerous practices that you think are not appropriate for others. Your child thinks what you do is okay, regardless of what you say.

Living a spiritually prosperous life is not only joyous and free, but actually the best service to others you can deliver.

5. Choose friends wisely.

Relationships, even casual ones, are often hurdles in life. But being connected to others is what life is all about. Children learn how to respect everyone, yet choose more valued relationships by watching their parents. Even when parroting their peers, they anchor their thinking in the observed practice of the adults in their lives. If they see prejudice, they will adopt intolerant ideas and views.

Children who have difficulty making friends need support and reinforcement. Otherwise, they will do anything for acceptance. Much the same holds true for adults who are candidates for chemical misuse or dependence.

6. Keep score.

It is important to know what your children read, watch, and do. Research demonstrates that monitoring a child's activities is an important way to lower his or her chances of getting involved in harmful or dangerous situations. Unsupervised children simply have more opportunities to engage in risky behaviors.

It is also important to observe and note isolating or unusual behavior by adults in the congregation who present signs of difficulty. This is particularly important when commitments are not met. This is not to "control" or judge the individual. It is simply a sign that appropriate responses are in order, whether greater involvement, special attention, or prayer are called for.

Those are the CSAT-recommended prevention practices. The Faith Partners experience has added two more.

7. Demonstrate faith.

Too often, people are careful to turn their difficulties over to God, yet keep the credit for the serendipities. Despite the brave front, others can usually somehow detect those who "walk the walk" as well as "talk the talk." Team members in a congregational ministry directed at addiction prevention and recovery bring an attitude of service and humility to the service as well as evidence peace, joy, and genuine fellowship.

The time-honored saying, "You can't give it away if you don't have it," is certainly true in congregations.

8. Congregate.

The power of congregating is one of the gifts of religious experience. These gatherings of people who share common religious beliefs provide an institutional space where it is safe for the individual to be vulnerable. Allowing one's self to be vulnerable is the beginning of self-examination, spiritual growth, and actual change in character and behavior.

In this safe and positive context, people share, mirror each other, serve each other, and teach each other. Traditional stories of faith presented through ritual prompt personal stories. People share examples of meeting challenges in the daily business of life.

In congregations, Faith Partners Team Ministries cross the spectrum of concern related to addiction and brokenness. The ministries channel the power of recovery through the congregation to nurture young people in the process of learning choice, context, and satisfactions. With a single message and a context of reinforcement, the teams help people at risk, people facing difficulty, and people in recovery.

This is prevention that works.

Twelve

Honoring the Fact and People of Recovery

We hoped for peace but no good has come,
For a time of healing but there was only terror.
Since my people are crushed, I am crushed;
I mourn, and horror grips me.
Is there no balm in Gilead?
Is there no physician there?
Why then is there no healing
For the wound of my people?

Jeremiah 8:15, 21-22

The great majority of successful recovery experiences include a profound spiritual renewal or "awakening" on the part of the individual. People re-connect, or in many cases connect for the first time, to a core personal relationship with a force deep within them. This relationship usually includes a belief system associated with that force. This belief system becomes a framework to successfully relate to the rest of humanity.

It seems to matter little what form or structure such a spiritual experience takes. For many, however, the experience leads to an earlier spiritual "home" – a religious tradition or heritage from childhood. This "homecoming" would seem natural, joyous, and productive for individuals and congregations. The story of the Prodigal Son illustrates the Christian version of this reunion.

In reality, however, this reunion is very often a tortured and dysfunctional relationship. People in recovery are often ready for the congregation, but the congregation and pastors may not be ready for them.

In many cases, individuals attend church in one part of town and Twelve Step meetings at churches in another part of town. They seldom acknowledge or discuss their addiction recovery experience in the congregation or worship.

In other cases, individuals discuss their recovery experience with a pastor or congregational leader, only to discover ignorance, judgment, and even resentment. They find another religious home in the faith tradition of their choice, but carefully avoid acknowledging their recovery again.

In yet other cases, individuals simply avoid religious institutions and build their own spiritual practice around friends and structures in the recovery community.

In far too few cases, the individual in recovery finds pastors and spiritual leaders who recognize the experience as part and parcel of the spiritual journey. In these cases, the individual finds welcome, joy, shared healing, and complete understanding. This understanding is not just based on the mental knowledge of addiction disease and recovery. It is based on the knowledge of human brokenness experienced by all and the universal experience that we heal together. In these situations, the individual in addiction recovery joins the healing process found in a healing congregation.

These are the "healing places" described in this book. No doubt increasing numbers of recovering people would turn to institutions of worship if they felt that the pastor and members understood recovery and were accepting, hospitable, and welcoming. The potential for healing at all levels is tremendous. The practice of non-judgmental acceptance and mutual healing is powerful. But the barriers to this potential are daunting.

How addiction is understood will determine the congregation's approach to people in recovery. The great majority of clergy and congregations view addiction through a narrow moral lens and the addiction experience as something that happens to others. Even when called upon to reach out, few identify their own susceptibility to addiction or own the people in the community who are afflicted or affected. The evidence clearly demonstrates that addiction is multidimensional, affecting the afflicted in physical, emotional, mental, and spiritual ways. This evidence seems to escape too many clergy and congregations – even as these faith leaders ponder how to be more relevant in a modern world.

Can clergy and congregations embrace knowledge of this disease that is beyond the control of the individual yet hold the alcoholic accountable for his or her behavior? More and more evidence suggests that the answer is positive and is, in fact, a key to greater service.

James B. Nelson, in his book, *Thirst: God and the Alcoholic Experience,* says that alcoholism is both a disease and an expression of sin's estrangement and brokenness. He says that people in recovery working the Twelve Steps are accustomed to confessing their sins in the form of making amends and attending to character defects. In the writer's experience with Twelve Steps there is little talk about disease, much more about taking personal responsibility for sobriety through a right relationship with God, confession, amends, forgiveness, and service to others.

Nelson further shares that understanding alcoholism as a disease markedly undercuts moralistic judgments and blaming, thus enhancing the chances for recovery. The affected are more likely to ask for help. The afflicted grant themselves some reprieve from their own judgment and begin the journey toward healing and health. This is a compelling reason for a shift in thinking. Even the attitude, "I don't understand alcoholism and I think I will withhold judgment until I do" is progress.

Because of this lack of understanding in and out of the church, shame penetrates every aspect and phase of the addiction continuum, especially recovery. And this is most unfortunate. This lack of understanding causes people to suffer for no reason. And their suffering has already been great.

The losses to the individual in recovery-the family and close associates-are staggering. People wear a permanent status of incomplete health, second-class citizenship, and diminished values in peer settings. Casting off this veil of untruth is extraordinarily difficult, even with the full knowledge that one is healed, forgiven, and at one with his or her God.

The losses accrue as well to the congregation, the community, the workplace, and society. Subjecting people to subtle punishment for addiction histories is not consistent with the science of addiction as a health concern and healing as both a physical and spiritual climb to wholeness. Administrators of shame lose as much as the objects of shame.

It is well to claim recovery, then, for the congregation, the community and society. Claiming recovery includes identifying with the illness, savoring the passage, and rejoicing in the victory.

How does the congregation claim recovery? How do the pastor and members identify with the illness? How can people of faith savor the passage and rejoice in the victory?

Research is clear about the impact of spiritual practices on healing and health. Those who are sick benefit from both good medical care and a caring, praying community. Many congregations are claiming their role through intercessory prayer and/or healing services. Just as we request prayers for an aunt about to have surgery, we can share that we are praying for close friends who are struggling with addiction. And just as we rejoice in the birth of an infant in the congregational family we can rejoice with the member who shares that he is celebrating his third sobriety birthday.

Congregations can claim recovery by making their community of faith a safe place for people to share the challenges of life, where people can be open and truthful, and where there are ongoing conversations about real life issues such as alcohol and other addictions. This will take awareness, education, appropriate referral information, and support for individuals and families. This book contains a process for developing a lay-led ministry that offers all of these things.

People of faith can make great strides against this illness by learning more about it. They can acknowledge that they, too, have family members who suffer with this disease. And even if they don't, they will discover that their lives have been affected by addiction. They will begin to see there is no "us and them." They will find that all of us seek answers outside ourselves. All of us run the danger of getting "hooked on" something other than the primary requirement of our faith – our mates, our jobs, our kids, money, position, to name a few.

John Keller, author of *Alcoholics and their Families: A Guide for Clergy and Congregations,* tells us that alcoholism becomes a paradigm for identification and getting a handle on the question, "What behavior in my life is providing relief from the brokenness and that foggy, anxiety-creating stuff in the common human condition?" He says it doesn't necessarily have to be an addiction. Anything that can change disease in our internal environment can be the expression of and have the potential for addiction. There is no way to know what might work for any given person, or why it does.

James Nelson offers that we need to go beyond transgressions of deed and character to the deeper stuff that realistically recognizes our alienation and brokenness in active addiction – from God, from our neighbors (family, community), and surely from ourselves. It is at this level that all people of faith can identify with the recovering person, for all fall short of keeping God in the center of their lives and hearts.

Finally, people of faith can savor the passage and rejoice in the victory by celebrating recovery at appropriate times and settings in the congregation.

Many of the Faith Partners Teams, along with doing awareness and education work with the pastor, have one worship service a year that acknowledges and celebrates recovery from addiction through written materials, prayers and liturgy, and personal testimonies.

In a congregation that has done this for several years, Cathy, co-chair of the special ministry, person in recovery, and speaker for the recovery worship service says, "Ultimately I stopped drinking because alcohol had begun to play too large a role in my life. However, it was not until I resumed going to church, began serving on the Faith Partners Team that my recovery came full-circle. Thanks in part to this ministry my life is finally integrated. I no longer have to be one person on Sunday and another every other day of the week. In many ways my life today is radically different. Part of that is attributable to my Twelve Step community, part of it to my children, but a very large part is due to my church and this ministry. For all of these things, as well as my continued sobriety I am extremely grateful."

"Whenever we offer acceptance, love, forgiveness, or a quiet word of hope, we offer health. When we share each other's burdens and joys, we become channels of healing. No matter how timid or tired, selfish or crazy, young or old, we all have something important to offer each other. Each of us is endowed by God with that gift of healing"
— Dr. Eric Ram, director of international health at World Vision

Henri Nouwen, author of the popular book *The Wounded Healer*, encourages those who minister to others to make their own wounded condition available to others as a source of healing. He says, "Service to others will not be perceived as authentic unless it comes from the heart wounded by the suffering of which he speaks."

This suggests that the healing power of congregation in the faith context requires much more than understanding gained through education and training, as desirable as that might be. A higher level of ownership is required for a higher level of power. Acceptance of the people and process of recovery can be conferred in specific acts of blessing. Such a congregational blessing is a ritual of faith, not a transfer of knowledge.

The faith community in our day has a unique opportunity to acknowledge and bless those who have been wounded by addiction so that they may become a blessing to others. What would it take for the church to not just be accepting of people in recovery but for the church to see them as gifts or blessings to the faith community? For surely, people in recovery have much to offer others. They have experienced great suffering and found meaning in it. They have walked a disciplined spiritual path. They have fallen on their knees and cried out to God, fully knowing that they cannot heal themselves.

Today, speaking from a Christian perspective, there is desire on the part of many within the church for authenticity, accountability, and a return to the passionate and sacrificial heartfelt faith and purpose of the early church. Likewise, there are a growing number of lay members who by combining their spiritual gifts with their life experience find purposeful and meaningful ministry to which they can commit themselves.

The new millennium has seen a tremendous new interest and focus on spirituality. For many, that simply translates to:

"Love God with all of your heart and your neighbor as yourself."

Wouldn't the church be enriched, strengthened, and even revitalized by the blessing of those who have walked the walk and are in a position to share their experience, strength, and hope with others? Wouldn't any faith community?

APPENDIX

Spiritual Awakening: How It Works

(The Twelve Steps of Alcoholics Anonymous)

Rarely have we seen a person fail who has thoroughly followed our path. Those who do not recover are people who cannot or will not completely give themselves to this simple program, usually men and women who are constitutionally incapable of being honest with themselves. There are such unfortunates. They are not at fault; they seem to have been born that way. They are naturally incapable of grasping and developing a manner of living which demands rigorous honesty. Their chances are less than average. There are those, too, who suffer from grave emotional and mental disorders, but many of them do recover if they have the capacity to be honest.

Our stories disclose in a general way what we used to be like, what happened, and what we are like now. If you have decided you want what we have and are willing to go to any length to get it—then you are ready to take certain steps.

At some of these we balked. We thought we could find an easier, softer way. But we could not. With all the earnestness at our command, we beg of you to be fearless and thorough from the very start. Some of us have tried to hold on to our old ideas and the result was nil until we let go absolutely.

Remember that we deal with alcohol—cunning, baffling, powerful! Without help it is too much for us. But there is One who has all power—that One is God. May you find Him now!

Half measures availed us nothing. We stood at the turning point. We asked His protection and care with complete abandon.

Here are the steps we took, which are suggested as a program of recovery:

1. We admitted we were powerless over alcohol—that our lives had become unmanageable.
2. Came to believe that a Power greater than ourselves could restore us to sanity.
3. Made a decision to turn our will and our lives over to the care of God *as we understood Him.*
4. Made a searching and fearless moral inventory of ourselves.
5. Admitted to God, to ourselves, and to another human being the exact nature of our wrongs.
6. Were entirely ready to have God remove all these defects of character.
7. Humbly asked Him to remove our shortcomings.
8. Made a list of all persons we had harmed, and became willing to make amends to them all.
9. Made direct amends to such people wherever possible, except when to do so would injure them or others.
10. Continued to take personal inventory and when we were wrong promptly admitted it.
11. Sought through prayer and meditation to improve our conscious contact with God *as we understood Him*, praying only for knowledge of His will for us and the power to carry that out.
12. Having had a spiritual awakening as the result of these steps, we tried to carry this message to alcoholics, and to practice these principles in all our affairs.

Many of us exclaimed, "What an order! I can't go through with it." Do not be discouraged. No one among us has been able to maintain anything like perfect adherence to these principles. We are not saints. The point is that we are willing to grow along spiritual lines. The principles we have set down are guides to progress. We claim spiritual progress rather than spiritual perfection.

Our description of the alcoholic, the chapter to the agnostic, and our personal adventures before and after make clear three pertinent ideas:

a) That we were alcoholic and could not manage our own lives.

b) That probably no human power could have relieved our alcoholism.

c) That God could and would if He were sought.

—*Alcoholics Anonymous*, pages 58-60. Twelve Steps reprinted with permission of Alcoholics Anonymous World Services, Inc. Permission to reprint this material does not mean that AA has reviewed or approved the contents of this publication nor that AA agrees with the views expressed herein. AA is a program of recovery from alcoholism only—use of the steps in connection with programs and activities, which are patterned after AA, but which address other problems, does not imply otherwise.

The Twelve Traditions

1. Our common welfare should come first; personal recovery depends upon AA unity.

2. For our group purpose there is but one ultimate authority—a loving God as He may express Himself in our group conscience. Our leaders are but trusted servants; they do not govern.

3. The only requirement for AA membership is a desire to stop drinking.

4. Each group should be autonomous except in matters affecting other groups or AA as a whole.

5. Each group has but one primary purpose—to carry its message to the alcoholic who still suffers.

6. An AA group ought never endorse, finance or lend the AA name to any related facility or outside enterprise, lest problems of money, property and prestige divert us from our primary purpose.
7. Every AA group ought to be fully self-supporting, declining outside contributions.
8. Alcoholics Anonymous should remain forever nonprofessional, but our service centers may employ special workers.
9. AA, as such, ought never be organized; but we may create service boards or committees directly responsible to those they serve.
10. Alcoholics Anonymous has no opinion on outside issues; hence the AA name ought never be drawn into public controversy.
11. Our public relations policy is based on attraction rather than promotion; we need always maintain personal anonymity at the level of press, radio and films.
12. Anonymity is the spiritual foundation of all our Traditions, ever reminding us to place principles before personalities.

Introduction to Faith Partners Teams

God of Liberation, it feels at time that our society is bound by things that enslave it. Unbind us and set us free to do your work in the world. Amen. May/June 1995, "Alive Now," The Upper Room.

From birth to death, through times joyous or filled with pain, our faith bears us up. Belonging to a congregation fills our need for community, gives us identity, and adds meaning to our lives. Faith communities offer us celebration and solace, spiritual growth and moral direction.

With calls and cards, casseroles and cakes, communities of faith shepherd us through the many transitions of life, including illness. Yet members of congregations all across this country suffer in loneliness and shame the physical, spiritual, and emotional ravages of addictive behaviors—their own and those of others.

We at the Rush Center of Johnson Institute recognize the threat alcohol and other drug misuse and addiction pose to the well being of individuals and families in our congregations. We know faith communities can play a unique role in supporting recovery from addictions and in preventing both use and abuse.

Rush Center and Faith Partners

Faith Partners, an organization founded by religious leaders from various faith traditions, has been working since 1996 to help faith communities prevent and reduce alcohol and other drug use problems among the people they serve. Over 100 congregations in four states have used the Faith Partners Team approach to organize members with special expertise, members who then educate the congregation, help hurting people find the resources they need, and support/celebrate recovery.

Now as a part of the Rush Center of Johnson Institute, the Faith Partners Team Ministry Approach is being introduced to new communities. Together we believe the basic issues involved in promoting health, in responding to those who suffer from addictions, and in preventing alcohol and other drug misuse are issues within the religious community's area of special expertise.

Call to Action

We at the Rush Center call on pastors and congregational leaders to join with recovering people and members of the larger community to provide a special ministry to people who suffer the effects of addiction. They need pastoral care as well as expressions of the divine love, which faith communities can offer.

We call on pastors and parents to join with other concerned adults to minister to the developmental needs of youth so that we might prevent their using alcohol or other drugs. Congregations must nurture young people morally and spiritually by offering them support, teaching them life and social skills, and talking with them honestly about the choices they face.

We call on all adult members of faith communities to support these ministries of recovery and prevention. We call upon them to become intentional about their own use of alcohol and other drugs and model responsible behavior, especially during times of transition such as new jobs, marriage, divorce, retirement, and bereavement. We call upon members to increase their understanding of addiction, its family dynamics, and the teachings of Alcoholics Anonymous and other Twelve Step programs.

We urge you to begin a team ministry in your congregation. There is something you can do to reduce alcohol and other drug use among young people and to support the recovery of those who suffer from their own addictions or those of others.

Vision and Promise

Our vision is of congregations across the country supporting members in their struggles to free themselves of addictions and put God

---

at the center of their lives. Our vision is of congregational families whose children live drug-free. We hope you will join us and we promise to help.

We will provide tools and guidance. We have developed strategies for building congregational teams to provide this team ministry within congregations. We can help you establish a team in your church by providing materials based on the experiences of dozens of teams, by supplying training and technical assistance, and by connecting you with a network of active addictions ministry teams.

Addiction Recovery Ministry Teams

The Rush Center has learned that developing a small group to work in addictions ministry increases the impact and makes the effort sustainable. That's why we advocate a team approach. A network of active addiction recovery ministry teams—in congregations large and small, urban and rural, in denominations from Baptist to Roman Catholic—now reaches across Texas and into Oklahoma, Ohio and Minnesota. They have undertaken numerous recovery/prevention activities, including:

- Teaching parents how to talk to their children about alcohol and other drugs;
- Taking people for assessments and helping them find treatment;
- Supporting family members;
- Bringing people in treatment to church for worship and study;
- Offering youth programs;
- Showing hospitality to Twelve Step programs;
- Starting scripture/Twelve Step study groups; and
- Tapping community resources to offer general educational programs.

Every team is different. How your ministry looks will depend on the general mission of your congregation and the needs of the community. It will also depend on your team's interests, gifts and energy. There is no right way to do this.

What is important is getting started!

Purpose and Scope of the Clergy Training Project

The Substance Abuse and Mental Health Service Administration (SAMHSA), part of the U.S. Department of Health and Human Services, joined with both the Johnson Institute (JI) and the National Association for Children of Alcoholics (NACoA) to explore ways in which the faith community can help address both the problems of alcohol and other drug dependence and the harmful impact these substance use disorders have on children and families. As part of that effort, the organizations sought to identify ways in which the topic could be incorporated into the education and training of clergy – ministers, priests, rabbis, deacons, elders, and pastoral ministers, such as lay ministers, religious sisters, among others.

To that end, in November 2001, SAMHSA supported a meeting of an expert panel on seminary education that was charged with the job of undertaking an assessment of the state of seminary training on the subjects of alcohol and other drug use and dependence. The panel found that seminary curricula and training programs vary extensively across the country, and few offer specific instruction focused on working with parishioners troubled with alcohol or drug use. With those findings, the panel recommended the development and implementation of a set of "core competencies" – basic knowledge and skills clergy need to help individuals and their families recover from alcohol and other drug use and dependence.

The panel concluded that a clergy training and curriculum development project was warranted and delineated a series of steps that should be taken to carry it forward. The goal: to enable clergy and other pastoral ministers to break through the wall of silence that surrounds alcohol and other drug dependence and to become involved actively in efforts to combat substance abuse and to mitigate its damaging effects on families and children.

Core Competencies

Core Competencies for Clergy and Other Pastoral Ministers In Addressing Alcohol and Drug Dependence and the Impact On Family Members

These competencies are presented as a specific guide to the core knowledge, attitudes, and skills essential to the ability of clergy and pastoral ministers to meet the needs of persons with alcohol or drug dependence and their family members.

1. Be aware of the:
   - Generally accepted definition of alcohol and other drug dependence
   - Societal stigma attached to alcohol and other drug dependence

2. Be knowledgeable about the:
   - Signs of alcohol and other drug dependence
   - Characteristics of withdrawal
   - Effects on the individual and the family
   - Characteristics of the stages of recovery

3. Be aware that possible indicators of the disease may include, among others: marital conflict, family violence (physical, emotional, and verbal), suicide, hospitalization, or encounters with the criminal justice system.

4. Understand that addiction erodes and blocks religious and spiritual development; and be able to effectively communicate the importance of spirituality and the practice of religion in recovery, using the scripture, traditions, and rituals of the faith community.

5. Be aware of the potential benefits of early intervention to the:
   - Addicted person
   - Family system
   - Affected children

6. Be aware of appropriate pastoral interactions with the:
   • Addicted person
   • Family system
   • Affected children

7. Be able to communicate and sustain:
   • An appropriate level of concern
   • Messages of hope and caring

8. Be familiar with and utilize available community resources to ensure a continuum of care for the:
   • Addicted person
   • Family system
   • Affected children

9. Have a general knowledge of and, where possible, exposure to:
   • The Twelve Step programs – AA, NA, Al-Anon, Nar-Anon, Alateen, A.C.O.A., etc.
   • Other groups

10. Be able to acknowledge and address values, issues, and attitudes regarding alcohol and other drug use and dependence in:
    • Oneself
    • One's own family

11. Be able to shape, form, and educate a caring congregation that welcomes and supports persons and families affected by alcohol and other drug dependence.

12. Be aware of how prevention strategies can benefit the larger community.